THE DISCIPLING CYCLE SERIES

Becoming Christlike
Leader's Guide

Andy and Kim Harrison
with Tara Vanarsdel

LifeWay Press
Nashville, TN

This book is the text for course number CG-0539 in the subject area
"Personal Life-Youth" of the Christian Growth Study Plan.

Dewey Decimal Classification: 248.83
Subject Heading: CHRISTIAN LIFE, TEENAGERS

Unless otherwise indicated, Scripture quotations are from the *New American Standard Bible*, © Copyright The Lockman Foundation, 1960, 1962, 1963, 1968, 1971, 1972, 1973, 1975, 1977.
Used by permission.

Scripture quotations marked (NIV) are from the Holy Bible,
New International Version. Copyright © 1973, 1978, 1984 by International Bible Society.
Used by permission.

Printed in the United States of America.
To order additional copies of this resource: WRITE LifeWay Church Resources Customer Service,
127 Ninth Avenue, North, Nashville, TN 37234-0113; FAX order to (615) 251-5933;
PHONE 1-800-458-2772; EMAIL to CustomerService@lifeway.com;
ONLINE at www.lifeway.com; or visit the LifeWay Christian Store serving you.

We believe that the Bible has God for its author; salvation for its end; and truth,
without any mixture of error, for its matter and that all Scripture is totally true and trustworthy.
The 2000 statement of *The Baptist Faith and Message* is our doctrinal guideline.

Youth Section
Discipleship and Family Group
LifeWay Christian Resources
of the Southern Baptist Convention
127 Ninth Avenue, North
Nashville, TN 37234-0152

CONTENTS

THE AUTHORS

Andy Harrison serves as Student Ministry and Education Specialist for the Baptist General Convention of Oklahoma. He assists churches in Oklahoma with youth Sunday School and Discipleship. Andy is a graduate of Oklahoma Baptist University and attended Southwestern Baptist Theological Seminary.

Andy and Kim ministered together on staff in the local church for nearly two decades, and it was during that time they developed The Discipling Cycle for their own students.

The Harrisons strongly believe that the years of adolescence are crucial in grounding students in the Word of God and in the spiritual disciplines of the faith. It is their hope that the curriculum provided in The Discipling Cycle will encourage Biblical discipleship in the church.

This book is dedicated to their children, Ted, Caleb, and Victoria.

FOREWARD

Jesus has commanded in the Great Commission to "Therefore go and make disciples of all nations, baptizing them in the name of the Father and of the Son and of the Holy Spirit, and teaching them to obey everything I have commanded you . . ." (Matt. 28:19-20a emphasis mine). Youth ministries in our country today have often failed at this task, not because the kids are unwilling, but because we as leaders have under challenged them. I have found that youth respond to a challenge more deeply and with greater sacrifice than any age group I know. With this shared conviction, Andy & Kim Harrison have developed The Discipling Cycle.

This book is more than a series of Bible studies, it is a pattern and plan for the challenge of youth discipleship. From the commitment to prayer for adult leaders to the one-on-ones with students, The Discipling Cycle presents a Christlike model for discipling youth. The Bible studies themselves are deeper in focus than much of the youth curriculum published today and consistently confront the student with Christ Himself.

The Discipling Cycle is designed to use the Word of God, prayer, and the consistent love of a discipling leader to challenge good students to become godly ones; ones able to internalize *2 Timothy 2:2, "And the things you have heard me say in the presence of many witnesses entrust to reliable men who will also be qualified to teach others."*

This program ought to be in every church and I challenge you to challenge your students and watch them grow *"in wisdom and stature, and in favor with God and men."*

Henry T. Blackaby

INTRODUCTION

The Discipling Cycle is a tool designed to help the youth minister or youth leader fulfill Jesus' Great Commission, "Go therefore and make disciples of all the nations, baptizing them in the name of the Father and the Son and the Holy Spirit, teaching them to observe all that I commanded you" (Matt. 28:19-20). The Discipling Cycle is ideal for the leader in search of material that will...

- strengthen the student's personal relationship with the Father through Jesus Christ,
- help students understand the longevity of the Christian walk,
- move students out of spectator seats and onto the playing field of evangelism,
- ground students in understanding theological issues,
- give methods for practical application of Scriptural truths,
- cultivate convictions for living a holy life.

The Discipling Cycle is a series of three books: **Becoming Christlike**; **Understanding God**; and **Seek, Share, Serve**. Each student book contains 30 weeks of Bible studies. A separate leader's guide gives easy-to-follow instructions for leading the 30 sessions. As students work through one book in the series, they should keep in mind that it is only one segment of a bigger picture. We are not called to know God without becoming like Him and sharing Him with the world. On the other hand, we cannot be like Him or effectively share Him until we know Him. This is why The Discipling Cycle series is most effective when taught as a whole and understood in the context of a three-year course. The purpose of each book is explained below.

Becoming Christlike helps believers understand who they are in Christ. As they understand that Christ's death, resurrection, holiness, and perfection apply to them, they will learn to live out those facts in their daily experience. They will examine specific elements of Christlikeness in each study, which will help them gain an overall picture of a holy life. We'll help students understand that God transforms the individual, enabling the believer to overcome sin and evil and to live a life of purity and holiness. Becoming

Christlike seeks to help in this transformation.

Understanding God helps believers know God. As students develop a desire and habit of personal, intimate time alone with God through prayer and Bible study, they will understand God as Father, Son, and Holy Spirit. Sessions focus on Bible study skill development. Students will look at the character of God and misconceptions about His character. (Available May 2001.)

Seek, Share, Serve focuses on evangelism and outreach as well as discipleship. You may want to make this book a prerequisite for local church ministry projects or summer mission trips. (Available May 2002.)

The books in this series are not sequential. Feel free to begin with any book in the series and call it "book one." If this is your first year to use The Discipling Cycle and Becoming Christlike is your choice to begin with, then next year students can continue the cycle with Understanding God. You don't need to begin new participants next year with Becoming Christlike; they simply may begin the cycle with Understanding God and then study Becoming Christlike the next time you offer it.

The Discipling Cycle asks for a commitment from students: (1) to the 30-week study, (2) to a 30-minute Bible study five days a week, and (3) to Scripture memory. This in-depth study motivates students to think.

No curriculum can make a disciple. Only people totally sold out to Christ and called out by Him should undertake discipling others through the power of the Holy Spirit. You must know that Christ called you, and you must know what that call looks like. Discipling an individual because you see the need for it is not enough. Discipling a student because you like him will set you up for disappointment. Becoming involved in this study because discipleship is the big emphasis in your church will prove to be a weak motivation. Jesus called us to make disciples, and He gave us a pattern of what that call looked like. He invested His life in the twelve for three years, and their lives impacted the world. If you want a ministry that looks like that, then you must understand that it is Jesus Himself who calls you to do it.

SCRIPTURE MEMORY

Scripture Memory is a vital part of the weekly studies. Get the students off to a good start by asking yourself now, "What are my convictions about Scripture memory?" Do you see it as a priority, or is it something you will go over if you have time? If you are not memorizing, your students will not memorize. This is one of those disciplines that is more caught than taught. You can preach sermons, sing hymns, or even assign a book on the subject; but if your students do not see you doing it, neither will they. (This goes for any discipline you are trying to pass on.)

The success of Scripture memory is not in how easily people memorize, but in how they use the verses in their lives. Your students will be able to pull off memorizing the weekly verse on the way to the discipleship meeting, and they will most likely be able to quote the verse. But ask them a week later what their verse was, and chances are they will have forgotten it—unless they see you set the example of applying the Scripture.

Giving youth choices—Each week's study in the student book has a boxed area entitled "Scripture Memory" at the top of the first page. Underneath it is a phrase which tells the topic. Below that are several Scripture references. The students choose one verse to memorize each week from the Scriptures listed. The verses' focus will always be on the topic being studied, although the topical phrase may vary a little from the study title.

Memorizing the verse—Memorize topic to reference and then reference to verse. Memorizing by topic will help students remember their verses for specific situations. Encourage them to spend extra time memorizing the reference and the first words of the verse. Usually, the first words are the most difficult to remember.

Reviewing—Go over and over the verses from previous weeks. When you review with your students, give only the topic. For example, say, "Teri, let me hear your verse on 'God's forgiveness.'" Then let her give you the reference and the verse. Allow the students to review you. Don't wait until you know the verses letter perfect. Let your students see your weaknesses as well as your strengths; they need to know that it requires discipline on your part as well as on theirs. Begin all your meetings with Scripture memory. Keep reviewing earlier verses. Do not let up. Understand up front that you will have difficulty keeping the majority of your students motivated in this area. You may be a one-voice cheering section. Don't get discouraged. Hang in there, and they will come to understand the value of Scripture memory.

Choosing the translation—Encourage students to memorize their verses from a Bible translation rather than from a paraphrase. You might want to suggest a translation to make it easier for students to work together and recite their verses together during the session. Students need to memorize the verses word for word. Leaving out a word or adding to the verse with extra words could change the meaning of the verse. (See Prov. 30:5-6.)

ONE TO ONES

At the heart of discipleship is meeting regularly with the students one to one at a time other than the discipleship group time. Set up an ongoing schedule with each student to meet with him or her individually. Talk with each student to determine what day and time will be best considering both your schedules. Weekly meetings are ideal, but meet with each student every two weeks if that is the best plan for your circumstances. Don't pressure yourself into doing more than what your priorities will allow. Be sensitive to God's leadership in determining what you will give in this area. Remember that as your Father, He is looking out for you as well as the students.

If you are the only one teaching this discipleship study and you have students of the opposite gender in your class, begin now to pray for someone who can help out with the other group (guys or girls). Schedule meetings only with those of the same gender and even then, in public places. Be creative. Would it be possible to meet during lunchtime at the student's school, or during break at her part-time job on the weekends?

If you begin to feel overwhelmed, remember that this is not your ministry but the Lord's. In reality, the issue is not how much time you can give but God's ability to minister through what time you can give. The burden is not on your shoulders to meet the needs of everyone. That burden belongs to God. If you can meet with each student only once every month or two, just remember that the dynamics of one-to-one time are life-changing, whenever you are able to meet.

USING TEAM LEADERS

If The Discipling Cycle group is less than 12 youth, you may be able to lead this study alone, with a person of the other gender handling the One to Ones with that gender. But if the group is larger than 12, you will most likely begin to feel overwhelmed when trying to carry out your responsibilities for the One to Ones. This section is written with this larger group of students in mind. If your group is small and you will be taking on the responsibilities of a Team Leader, you may want to read the job description that follows.

Keep your eyes open for potential disciple-makers, but remember God is the One who will be directing other adults to you. Your job is to pray for other adults willing to be students learning along with the teenagers and called to minister to teenagers through the One to Ones. Then be open and encouraging of other adults joining the group.

As coordinator of this ministry, consider yourself a "shepherd" of your adult helpers. Consider each adult's schedule, temperament, and stamina. Listen to what the Team Leaders say and determine for which students God seems to have given them a specific heart. You are, in a sense, responsible for the well-being of your disciple-makers. Ask them how many students they think they can handle. Consider recent stress factors that may have surfaced in their lives lately: a new spouse, a new baby, a new position in some other ministry within your church, and so forth. Ask God for a sensitivity to

their personal situations and especially to their own feedback regarding what they can handle.

Job Description for the Team Leader

At the heart of discipleship is meeting regularly with the students one to one at a time other than the discipleship group time. As the Team Leader, you are responsible to meet one to one only with the guys or girls on your team. Set up an ongoing schedule with each student to meet with him or her individually. Talk with each student to determine what day and time will be best considering both your schedules. Weekly meetings are ideal, but meet with each student every two weeks if that is the best plan for your circumstances. Don't pressure yourself into doing more than what your priorities will allow. Be sensitive to God's leadership in determining what you will give in this area. Remember that as your Father, He is looking out for you as well as the students.

During these meetings, work on Scripture memory first since it is the easiest thing to put off to the point that it never gets done. Remember to let the student review you on your verse. In the beginning, students may be rather quiet, so be prepared to ask questions to draw them out. Listen for what is burdening them, whether at home or school, with dating or other relationships. Remember your own high school experiences in relating with the students. Ask them specifics about their Bible studies, especially questions that ask for their opinion, such as, "Which Scripture spoke the most to you from last week's study?" or "Which question really made you think and why?" Ask for their opinions and input in regard to the large group discussion time. They are eager to give it. Of course, make it a priority to spend time in prayer during each meeting. Ask the student to pray for your requests as well as your praying for the student. Some are less reserved than others. Some will find it hard to not tell you the things they think you want to hear. Every person is different, and wisdom in bringing down a person's guard only comes from God. So ask Him (James 1:5).

Following are pointers to keep in mind when developing a relationship with the students on your team:

INITIATE

The Lord initiated a relationship with us through His Son. Follow His example by being the initiator in relationships with the students on your team.

- When you see students who are on your team, don't wait for them to approach you, go up to them.
- Don't wait for him or her to contact you; contact the student.
- Find time to have fun with the students on your team.
- Look for opportunities to get on their turf. Go watch them play in a game, take them shopping.
- Don't think that taking the initiative is a one-time effort.

Call them, send encouraging notes, continue to set up times to meet even if they skip their One to Ones. Decide now on your role as initiator for the entire study, regardless of whether they ever initiate anything with you.

CULTIVATE

A farmer cultivates the seed so it can grow, protecting it and nourishing it. Through all of his efforts, his vision is not on the seed but rather on what the seed will become. Ask the Lord to give you vision for what each of your students will become. He is so faithful to let you see if you ask Him. He already sees the finished result: their perfection in Christ. You need to see this too. "For in due time we shall reap if we do not grow weary" (Galatians 6:9).

AFFECTION-ATE

People need to be loved and feel loved. You will be amazed at how your genuine love impacts the students on your team. Communicate your love in many creative, appropriate ways.

EDUCATE

Let the students on your team know you are a disciple, too. (The word disciple means "learner.") Place more emphasis on what God is teaching you than on what you think you need to teach them. They are learning much more from what you do than from what you say. Let them see you working on Scripture memory. Let them see your burden for lost people. Let them see your heart. There are so many ways you can teach without ever formally "teaching." Do not be afraid to let them observe your life: strengths and weaknesses.

COMMUNICATE

Learn to be the kind of communicator who puts others at ease. Ask good questions. Be a good listener, even if what they talk about is trivial to you. Do not make the student feel uncomfortable or "stupid" because he or she could not think of anything to say. Don't take it personally if a student does not spill his or her whole life story by the third time you have met. It takes time to earn the role of confidant.

IMITATE

Give students a picture of what Jesus is like. Simply be an imitator of Jesus in all that you do, and the Lord will use your life to impact many.

THE WEEKLY SESSION

Schedule the sessions practically. Here's the schedule we suggest for your weekly meetings:

Team Meetings (20 minutes)
Large-group Discussion (40-50 minutes)
Team Leaders Meeting (15 minutes)

TEAM MEETINGS

The small group time is led by the Team Leaders. During this time, the Team Leaders carry out the following functions each week. You might want to duplicate these to hand each Team Leader.

Touch base—Take a little time in team meetings to continue establishing relationships. Let the students know that you care about the details: tests, their dating lives, their relationship with their parents. Be sure to budget your time.

Accountability—Using a form such as that on page 12, record attendance, how many days each student completed in the Student Edition, and which verse the student chose to memorize. Recording this information will help you evaluate whether a student is struggling. For instance, if a student hasn't completed a single day of the studies for two weeks, then you may want to get with the student and complete a day or two of Bible studies together in the next week. This will help you understand if the student is struggling with understanding the studies or just needs perspective on priorities. As students struggle with their performance, they'll be tempted to quit. Always remember to give them a picture of what Jesus is like. Communicate to the student that your desire is not to get him or her to perform but to help in his or her relationship with the Lord.

Scripture Memory—Ask students to pair up to review their Scripture memory verse. Encourage them to review old verses. This could and even should begin each meeting. As students come in, they can immediately begin reviewing. Quote your verse for the students as well. To reinforce students' commitment to memorization, ask youth to recite the verses aloud together. If several haven't memorized the same verse, they may be hesitant to do this. Make this a fun, guilt-free experience.

Prayer—Take prayer requests and encourage team members to pray aloud. This is something they need to become comfortable doing.

LARGE-GROUP DISCUSSION

As the Study Leader, you lead this discussion as the rest of the adults and the students give their input. Once again, budget your time, encourage discussion, and leave them hungry for more.

In preparation for the study each week, flag the questions and activities you sense are priorities for discussion. Allow time at the end for questions from the students. Encourage the Team Leaders' input in helping answer the students' questions at this time.

TEAM LEADERS MEETING

Make this a time of prayer and encouragement. Use passages such as Matthew 28:19-20; Colossians 1:28-29; 2 Timothy 2:2; John 15:4; and John 12:24-26 to remind them of their purpose and from whom their strength comes. Use principles from the "Job Description for the Team Leader" as a point of reference. Ask them how they are doing with their One to Ones. Review the weekly progress of the students by going over the Accountability Sheets filled out by the Team Leaders.

Discuss difficult-to-handle situations, such as an isolated problem with one of the students. Ask the leaders for their input regarding the large-group time. Plan a party outside the discipleship time for all the adults and their spouses. Love one another. Support one another.

COMMON QUESTIONS

What is the best way of recruiting students for this study?

Students must make the decision to participate in The Discipling Cycle for themselves. Encouragement from home, you, or anyone else is important. But pushing youth into doing the study will be counterproductive.

Make recruiting a year-round event. Begin with prayer. Pray for new members of the youth group and their possible participation in the study when you begin a new book. From time to time, speak to the new members about what they are doing in regard to discipleship. Communicate that you would like them to be a part of the study next year. Be sure to mention the commitment involved.

Your present members will be your best recruiters. Suggest students excited about the study encourage their friends to join, too. Be open to the students bringing friends from other churches.

Can youth join the study after it is already underway?

Since the studies build upon each other week by week, this series is not designed to be an "open class" where students can join at any time. Just as Jesus focused His attention on the twelve, consider The Discipling Cycle group a core group that takes time and effort to disciple. Your youth group needs to have ministries that reach the crowd, just as Jesus spent time with the multitudes, but this resource is not intended for that purpose. (Check out Tm4•1•2 for a crowd resource.)

Upon what criteria should we base our selection of Team Leaders?

The position of Team Leader is key to your success. This position should be held by someone who is willing to be a learner and a servant, who will exercise patience and forbearance, and who sees the value of accountability. The Team Leader should be an adult worker (perhaps a mature college student) who desires to grow and who senses God calling him or her to become a disciple-maker.

How can we expect students to hang in there for 30 weeks when they don't hang in for 6 to 8?

The question is really not whether students will hang in there for 30 weeks, but rather will you? If you continue to love, support, and encourage students and remain faithful to meeting with them one to one, they will be there in the end.

Can a non-Christian be included in this study as a means to encourage him or her to accept Christ?

No. This study is for those who have previously made a commitment to Christ and want to grow in respect to that decision. The Bible studies do not include an evangelistic appeal to students regarding salvation.

Should I ever encourage a student to drop out of The Discipling Cycle?

Some students will not memorize one verse. Some will never complete all five days of a particular study. Expect this. When you have exhausted all prayers, personal helps, and efforts and the student still is not responding, then consider speaking with him or her about continued participation. Sometimes a student just does not want what you are offering. God will have to bring the student to a point of desire. Remember two things: (1) always examine your own devotion to make sure you have been obedient to God in regard to that student and (2) let the student know that dropping the course does not mean that you no longer care about the student.

If a student in your group has a blatantly sour attitude and his attitude is hindering and/or discouraging other students, then you will need to go to that person individually. Tell the student that his attitude is benefiting no one. Ask the student if he could make a more conscious effort to be a positive leader in the class. If his attitude remains unchanged, you will have to ask the student to drop the course.

Should the adult Team Leader memorize all three verses assigned to each week's study?

No. Nothing is gained by super feats of memorization. The Team Leader need only memorize one verse just like the students.

Should the students remain with the same Team Leader all three years?

No. The students, as well as the Team Leaders, need to realize that Christ is the focus and not any other individual.

What do I do when the students in the group begin to display a lack of motivation?

Use those times to teach. Paul probably was not motivated every day and every moment, yet he hung in there. Teach the students that the race is a marathon, not a sprint. You might win a sprint on emotions, but you most assuredly will not win a marathon on them.

How long should a One to One last?

The time is not as significant as the content. Make time for reviewing Scripture verses, praying, and listening. The time could range from 20 minutes to three hours. Be sincere and be yourself.

What should we do after the 30-week study until we move on to the next book?

Enjoy a break. Periodically check on youth to see how they are using the things they learned. Get the group together for a fun activity, perhaps a day trip to an amusement park.

YEARLY SCHEDULE

Planning the 30-week study to occur during the standard school calendar months work well. The summer months are a natural break during which the students are free to go on scheduled mission trips, with their family on vacations, and to assorted camps. Here's one schedule you might consider:

- Kickoff Party...............................August
- September-November ....13 meetings
- Thanksgiving—New Year's Day ..Christmas Break
- January—Early May.....................17 meetings
- May – August ....Summer Break

Kickoff Party

Invite all interested students and Team Leaders to come to your house or the church for dinner and fellowship in late August. At this gathering, explain The Discipling Cycle and the commitment involved. Look through the books together and explain the five-day study set-up and the time required. By coming to the Kickoff Party, youth are not joining the Discipleship group, they are only hearing the facts so they can decide whether or not to join. This should be a fun event which serves as an opportunity to enlist and inform students.

Kickoff Party Checklist:
- ❏ Send out notes to potential participants. Include "when" and "where" information and emphasize that attending the party is not a commitment to join.
- ❏ Have books available to hand out to the students who are certain that they want to make the commitment.
- ❏ Arrange for food.

The First Meeting

Sometime between the kickoff party and the first meeting, get a verbal commitment from individuals who are going to participate. Once you have commitments, assign each student to a Team Leader of the same gender. Make up a schedule of the year to hand out to students at the first meeting, noting those days when you will not meet. Ensure you have enough books on hand to give each student. Ensure each student has an easily understandable Bible translation, not a paraphrase.

ACCOUNTABILITY SHEET

Team Leader's Name_____

DATE	STUDENTS PRESENT	DAYS COMPLETED	VERSE SELECTED

You may duplicate this form for use within your church.

HOW TO USE THIS LEADER'S GUIDE

The sessions in this Leader's Guide provide you, the Study Leader, with questions, life situations, activities, and analogies that extend the concepts youth have encountered in the weekly studies. Their purpose is to engage students in applying the concepts learned.

Sessions are organized by the day of the study in the Student Edition (Day 1, Day 2, etc.). Read and work through the Student Edition each week before planning the session. Consider all questions and activities in the Leader's Guide optional. Choose the suggestions for each day that you sense to be a priority for discussion. The sessions include the following standard elements:

 **FOCUS**

A focus statement is given for each day's study. It restates the concept(s) the students should have learned from completing the activities in the Student Edition.

 **APPLICATION**

Questions are the main method of teaching this study. The questions are usually related to the daily Bible study in the Student Edition. Numbers beside the questions clearly identify the corresponding sections in the Student Edition. All sections of the Student Edition will not be discussed during the session. Address the questions to the large group and encourage students to participate in the discussion that follows. Following each question are suggested answers and/or points you need to make. If student answers will vary because of the subjectiveness of the question, the phrase "Possible answers" will precede the text.

You will notice various things about the questions related to the Student Edition sections:

- Questions not preceded by a number are based on the same number as the previous question.
- Questions based on Scripture references will be designated by the particular reference.
- Questions based on commentary included in the Student Edition will be preceded by the first words of the paragraph.
- Questions based on a particular quotation from the study are referred to by the last name of the writer of the quotation.

In addition to questions pertaining to sections in the Student Edition, sessions may include the following elements:

 LIFE SITUATION

This symbol indicates a story to be read aloud to the small group. The story corresponds to a concept from the Student Edition, which will be clearly noted with a number or partial quote from the study. These stories, when combined with the questions for discussion which follow, will help youth apply the concepts to their lives.

 ACTIVITY

This symbol precedes an activity that may be at the beginning of the study, at the end of the study, or in the middle of the study following a question or a quotation to which it relates. These activities are approximately five minutes in length. Most activities will require either pencil and paper or a dry-erase board.

 DISCUSSION

This symbol precedes discussion questions intended to focus students' attention on the concepts to be learned in the upcoming study. These questions don't relate specifically to particular sections in the Student Edition, but rather to the topic for the week in general. You make the choice of whether to use them at the end of the previous session, during the week in your One to Ones, at the beginning of the session, at the end of the session after the study has been completed to review general concepts, or not at all.

The questions and activities suggested for each session require time to adequately complete and discuss. Therefore, you must review the questions and activities prior to the discipleship session and determine which ones would be of particular value to the specific group, limiting the discussion and activities to those that are most applicable.

WEEK 1
THE NEW LIFE

 DISCUSSION

How do you feel when you think of getting something that is brand new, never been used before, and completely perfect?

Possible answers: Excited. It's nice to have something that no one else has "messed up."

How do you feel when you think about having a brand new life?

Possible answers: Optimistic regarding the future. It's encouraging not to have to remember the past and its mistakes. Grateful to have a new start.

DAY 1

 FOCUS

God's will is that we be Christlike. Jesus is the model of what God intended for all of humanity to be like. A Christian is a new creature and therefore must reject the old life, which was crucified with Christ, in favor of the new one, which is raised in Him.

 APPLICATION

1. How did you feel after filling in this section?

Possible answers: Overwhelmed. Like this is impossible. How can I love as Christ loves?

Assure students that it is normal to feel this way and that this study will help them understand how they can become Christlike.

6. People could be fooled into believing something is new when it is actually old. For example, a new paint job and the "new car smell" sprayed into a used car could fool some. How could this be applied to a person who only seems to have the new life?

A person can appear to have the new life when in fact he or she doesn't. People can imitate Christian actions, attitudes, and motives; but a person can be truly transformed into Christ's likeness only after being "born again."

8. What kind of interests would a dead corpse have? Would it be interested in sin? Earthly pleasures? Worldly gain?

A dead corpse wouldn't have any interests.

What kind of rights would a dead corpse have? The right to live it up once in a while? The right to have its "needs" met? The right to indulge itself?

Likewise, a dead corpse does not have any rights.

If we have been crucified with Christ, where must our interests lie? What rights do we have?

Our interests must be in Him alone and in the desire to be like Him. We must give Him all control.

LEWIS QUOTATION

If we work hard enough at it for a long enough period of time, will we be able to be someone who shares God's power, joy, knowledge, and eternity?

It's not a matter of working hard. We do not work to become Christlike. But as we submit to God's will and allow Him to be in control of our lives, we will become more like Him. We won't have to work at it. Through His grace, we will just become it.

DAY 2

 FOCUS

Jesus told the parable of tearing up a new garment in order to patch an old garment. It is impossible to patch the old life with pieces of the new. We must completely reject the old life with its enslavement to sin in favor of the brand new life we have in Him. Continuing to choose the ways of the old life will cause us to forget who we really are in Christ.

 APPLICATION

11. How is cutting up a brand new pair of pants and using the pieces to patch the holes in an old pair being wasteful?

You are ruining not only the brand new pair of pants but also the old ones since the patches won't match and will shrink when washed.

13. How do many people, including Christians, see Christianity in terms of having Jesus there to "fill in the holes" of their lives?
They don't allow Him to take the lead in their lives daily. They see Him as a "safety net" to call upon when they need divine intervention.

When Christians live this kind of lifestyle, they may occasionally turn their faces toward Jesus, but how are they treating Him most of the time?
They are turning their backs on Him.

Who are we considering more important when we give Jesus fragments of our lives?
Ourselves

When we opt for a new life all together, who is more important?
Jesus. We maximize His importance and minimize our own.

14. What is the difference between embracing only pieces of Christlikeness and totally replacing the old nature?
When we embrace only pieces of Christlikeness, we generally choose those requiring little sacrifice, those easiest to achieve, or those most convenient to change. As we allow our old nature to die completely, the total change will take place over time, at first only for moments as described by C. S. Lewis. Those first moments of determined, sacrificial change are the first steps toward complete surrender to Christ.

When we choose to obey God, we are releasing His power to work in our lives that enables us to overcome the temptations of the old life. When we choose to give in to those temptations and opt for the old life, whose power are we actually releasing to work in our lives?
We are leaving ourselves open and vulnerable to the attacks of Satan.

18. Continuing to live out the old life when we have been given a new life is like the boy who was raised by a pack of wolves for the first few years of his life. When found by humans and brought into a normal home, the boy didn't want to sit in a chair and use silverware to eat a meal placed before him. Instead, he tried to catch the cat so he could eat him. How are
these situations similar?
Although he was obviously a human, he was more comfortable acting like what he was not—a wolf. If we choose to continue to live out the old life, it is because we choose to do so. We are more comfortable being what we are not than living out what we actually are.

DAY 3

FOCUS
Because the characteristics of the old life will incur God's wrath, we are to lay aside the old life with its evil practices. To put on the new self is to put on Christ and the characteristics and deeds that make up the new life in Him. Exposing ourselves to His Word and His teachings will positively impact the new life. Allowing Christ to be Lord of our lives means we allow Him to live through us so that we may glorify Him.

APPLICATION

LIFE SITUATION
21. Gary dated Cindy for several months. During that time, he accumulated many things that he associated with their relationship: photographs, gifts, their "song," old notes, and cards. But when the relationship ended painfully, Gary found it necessary to rid himself of all those things. He cut up old pictures, returned her class ring, and tossed out old cards and gifts. He got rid of everything he had that reminded him of Cindy. Why?
Possible answers: It can be painful to hold on to a lost relationship. He has to get on with your life. Living in a past that doesn't exist anymore will make him miserable.

How would your new boyfriend or girlfriend feel if you kept pictures and mementos of your previous relationship on display?
It would certainly cause problems with him or her. Your new relationship would not have the chance to succeed.

How does this parallel the necessity of giving up our old lifestyle in favor of our new life in Christ?
If we cling to certain aspects of the old life at the same time we are attempting to experience a new life with Christ, we'll never experience the incredible joy Christ offers us. The old cannot be mixed with the new. Conflict will result.

When you think of putting on...
You are wearing a shirt and a pair of pants. Outside, a blinding snowstorm is raging. Six inches of snow is on the ground, and there is no sign of the storm letting up any time soon. So before you walk outside in your shirt and slacks, you put on a pair of gloves. No hat. No jacket. No socks or shoes. Just a pair of gloves. How successful will you be at staying warm?
You will be dangerously cold. Your gloved hands won't even be warm because the rest of your body is not protected.

If we clothe ourselves with only pieces of Christ, what do we accomplish?
Nothing. Because are not clothing ourselves with all of Him, we are leaving ourselves unprotected.

25. What is likely to happen to the new life that does not fellowship with believers, become established in a church, or read the Bible and pray?
It will quickly opt for the old life.

What if a Christian strives to live out the new life in order to gain the favor of Christian friends?
This is an improper motive. The purpose of the new life is to glorify Christ, not achieve any personal glory or gain. The person who seeks to "live right" for reasons other than glorifying God will probably fall back into the old pattern of life.

DAY 4

 FOCUS
We must choose daily to walk the path of righteousness, humility, and love. When we choose to obey God, our hearts are softened, bent toward Him, and able to understand Christ's teachings and what He experienced. As we cultivate our relationship with Him, God reveals more of Himself to us.

 APPLICATION
29. Why is it impossible to walk down the path of sin and the path of righteousness at the same time?
For the same reason that it would be impossible to physically walk down two different streets at the same time. You have to make a choice regarding which street you will walk along. The same is true of the path of sin and the path of righteousness. If you are walking down the right path but then choose to sin, you are no longer walking down the street of righteousness. You have taken a detour.

30. Do you think people who have chosen to live a life of sin—whether as career criminals, drug dealers, slanderers, or thieves—give much thought to spiritual matters? Why is that?
No. They seem to live a life completely apart from God. Their choices have excluded them from the life of God. Their hearts are hardened so that they likely do not even give Him a thought.

32. Indicate the world's response in regard to Christ's teaching:

Jesus says...
Be humble, regarding others as more important than yourself.
The world says...
If you do that, you're just a doormat.
Jesus says...
Turn the other cheek.
The world says...
Then people will take advantage of you.
Jesus says...
Love those who don't love you.
The world says...
You'll be wasting your time on someone who doesn't even care about you.
Jesus says...
Be willing to suffer for doing what is right
The world says...
The most important thing is for others to accept you and like you, so be willing to compromise.

The world does not understand why Jesus teaches us to live a life of humility. What do you think happens in the life of a Christian when he or she begins to put Christ's teaching into practice? What does he or she then begin to understand about Jesus?
The new life's response is to be taught and to listen. When we obey Christ's teachings, we begin to understand why Jesus instructs us to do these things and what He experiences every day. He loves those who do not love Him; He suffered for doing what was right.

34. What do you think happens to the heart of a person who obeys even when he or she doesn't necessarily want to?
His or her heart softens as he or she becomes receptive to what the Lord has to teach. For example, you may not have wanted to attend this discipleship session or go to church Sunday morning; but God will teach you things through these experiences that you will use the rest of your life.

35. What is the result of obeying and walking in the pattern of the new life?

You will continue to grow in your knowledge and understanding of God.

DAY 5

 FOCUS

Sin enslaves those who choose to follow after it. We do not need to do what is right in order to earn God's favor. We live righteously because, as His children, we already have His favor. Transformation is God's purpose for those who have been saved.

 APPLICATION

37. We are easily fooled into thinking that sin serves us. Sinning brings excitement and often acceptance to us. But Jesus teaches about the deceitfulness of sin. What is actually true about sin in our lives?

Sin doesn't serve us. Instead, we become its servant. If we allow it to, it will own us. The most obvious example of this is drug addiction. A less obvious example is gossiping. We might begin by speaking negatively about an individual in a certain situation but eventually end up having a negative outlook and speaking negatively about others in general.

39. God saved us because He loves us. What should be our motivation for living as He would have us live?

Our love for Him. "If you love Me, you will keep My commandments" (John 14:15).

40. Which reason for doing right would make you feel enslaved to doing right? Which would make you feel free to do right?

Doing right in order to earn God's favor makes you enslaved to righteousness, which can be as stifling as being enslaved to sin. You will quickly find that you can never do enough. But understanding that as His child you already please Him, you are free to walk in righteousness. God is transforming you, not judging your every move to see how righteous you appear to be. You aren't trying to earn anything.

If you were a billionaire, why might you choose to work at a job anyway?

Possible answers: Because I enjoy the work. Because the work is fulfilling.

WEEK 2
BECOMING WHO YOU ALREADY ARE

DAY 1

FOCUS

Our goal as Christians is to die to our old self and press on toward our new identity in Christ. In his letter to the Philippians, Paul wrote of this righteousness in Christ being both a goal we as believers have already attained and a goal for which we are striving. Because we have accepted Christ, we have attained perfection in Christ; but at the same time we are pressing on daily toward the finish line: complete unity with Christ.

APPLICATION

2. We think of a goal as something we strive for, something that is important to us, something that will make us feel successful. The goal Paul refers to here is different. What do you think is the focus of this goal?
What is valuable to God. What He would have us to be.

7. Striving to reach a goal that we have already attained may not seem to make sense. However, can you think of situations in life where someone might actually be striving to attain a goal that he has already reached?
Possible answers: Striving to break the world record in a specific race for which you are the world record holder. Receiving a college diploma that says you are a physician but then having to work to set up a practice in order to actually become one. An Academy Award winner seeking to win another Academy Award.

DAY 2

FOCUS

Our old life has been buried with Christ, and a new life is resurrected in Him. These are facts that do not change regardless of our performance or emotions. We are only able to experience the new life when we understand the facts of our righteousness in Him.

APPLICATION

9. Name facts you know to be true about the life Jesus led while He was on earth.
Possible answers: He never sinned. He was compassionate. He loved others. He served others.

10. We know that we died to sin and were raised to righteousness in Him. Based on the attributes of Christ mentioned in question 9, what is also true of yourself, based on God's perspective of you?
We are also sinless, compassionate, servants, we love others, etc.

11. Once we accept Christ, we are no longer a slave to sin. As Christians, why do we continue to sin?
We sin because we choose to sin.

12. What is typically done with a corpse? Is it kept around for long? How is the inevitable destination of a corpse like the old life?
A corpse is buried. The old life, too, is buried or destroyed. We no longer interact with it.

LEWIS QUOTATION

Why are we not truly "ourselves" until we turn to Christ?
When we become Christians, we cease to live apart from Christ; He actually lives within us. "I have been crucified with Christ; and it is no longer I who live, but Christ lives in me" (Gal. 2:20).

When you consider the physical birth...

LIFE SITUATION

Leon is a Christian who is struggling with sin in his life. He wants to feel the same closeness to God he felt during church camp. But lately he feels distanced from God. He knows he should stand up for Kenny, the guy everyone on the team calls a "wimp." But Leon just can't seem to go against the crowd. He wants to be more patient with his little brother, but it's so hard not to get mad at him when he does things purposely to make Leon mad. He has a burden for his lost friend, but he can't get up the courage to talk to him about Christ. And the list goes on and on. Leon feels defeated. He doesn't see how he can possibly accomplish those things he knows he should be doing.

Why is Leon experiencing so much defeat even in the midst of his "new life"?
He is experiencing defeat because he is not acknowledging the fact of his resurrection to a new life. He is basing his level of success or failure as a Christian on his emotions and on his performance. Jesus wants us to live and view our lives according to the facts.

NEE QUOTATION
"Of course I don't believe the world is round. If it were, we'd fall off the bottom of it!"
"I don't think they really meant to kill their parents. They just got caught up in their rage."
"I believe we could live for months without water."
"Yeah, they showed pictures of men on the moon. But I think it was just a big gag scientists pulled on the whole world, and the whole world believed it!"

What makes these statements seem ridiculous?
The opinions of these people do not change the facts. The world is round whether someone believes it or not. Whether people meant to kill their parents or not does not change the fact that they are dead. Believing you could live for months without water and actually doing it are two completely different things. Thinking men on the moon was a hoax doesn't change the fact that men were actually there.

Why are the facts of the new life so important?
Because they're facts. They won't change regardless of our feelings, successes, or failures. We are no longer slaves of sin. In the new life, we are instruments of righteousness whether we feel righteous or not.

Why must you understand...

Before we can truly experience righteousness, what must we understand about ourselves?
That in Christ we are righteous.

Before we can truly show compassion, what must we understand about ourselves? Before we can demonstrate selflessness? Before we can have patience? Before we display unconditional love?
We must realize that in Christ we already are compassionate, selfless, patient, and loving.

Many Christians don't experience the new life because they don't understand what God has put into their account. Others believe the amount in the account constantly changes. For example, someone may not experience $500 because he doesn't know it's there. Another person may think her account balance varies according to her feelings or her sin. She misses church several weeks in a row and believes her account goes down to $400. She gripes about her sister for getting into her jewelry and thinks her account goes down to $375. She tells her mother she made an A on her science project when she really made a C—down to $200. But, she invites her lost friend to a youth rally, so her balance goes up to $250. **If you shared this girl's view, how would this prevent you from experiencing the new life?**
You would believe your "account balance" is dependent on what you put into it, not on what Christ put there. Your new life would be based on your performance instead of a result of what He did and His grace. We need to understand that we actually have unlimited funds in our account that can never be reduced. Only then will we be able to experience our riches.

DAY 3

 ACTIVITY
Make two columns on chart paper or a marker board. Write the Characteristics of Jesus (listed below) in one column. Title the other column, Characteristics of Me. Ask students to suggest answers for that column. Record answers. Possible answers are given below.

Characteristics of Jesus
His thoughts and motives are pure.
He loves unconditionally.
He serves.
He is selfless.
His words edify.
His patience knows no limits.

Characteristics of Me

My thoughts and motives are impure.
I often love based on whether someone is worthy.
I usually prefer to be served.
I am selfish.
My words often degrade.
I can remain patient for only so long.

 **FOCUS**

Second Corinthians 5:21 tells us that our sinful life has been exchanged for Christ's sinless life. We have become the righteousness of God in Him. Because you have been freely given this status through God's grace, we can seek to live up to what we have already attained in our daily experience without becoming weary.

19. Hebrews 10:14 says, "For by one offering He has perfected for all time those who are sanctified." Since we have been perfected in Christ, what words could describe the way God sees us now?
Possible answers: blameless, sinless, holy, righteous, kind, gentle, patient, compassionate, pure, sincere, etc.

ARTHUR QUOTATION

Just as believing what God says about us makes us eager to serve the Lord, what does not understanding or even not believing what God says about us have the potential to do?
Not believing God can make us feel inadequate, stifled, and defeated. We may not be eager to serve the Lord because we may see it as a means to gain His favor, which is defeating in itself. We may become discouraged and lose hope in our ability to serve Him.

21. If you were learning how to play the piano and every time you hit one wrong note in your 12-page concerto you had to start all over again, how would you feel about learning to play the piano?
Possible answers: discouraged, frustrated, impatient, nervous

How would you feel if you were just learning how to read and every time you pronounced a word wrong you had to start the book over?

What if you had to complete dozens of pages of math problems but had to work all of the problems over again every time you missed one?

What is the significance of having an exchanged, perfect life in terms of your motivation to live up to what you have already attained?
Possible answers: Knowing that I don't have to "start over" whenever I stumble is such a blessing. I won't grow weary in doing good because I'm not trying to earn something through it. It leaves me free to pursue a life of righteousness.

DAY 4

 FOCUS

As Christians, we are God's chosen people, a royal priesthood, a holy nation. Having a clear understanding of who and what we already are encourages us to live it out in our everyday lives.

APPLICATION

23. If you don't have a finished product to refer to as you are making a craft or project, how could this affect your attitude about the work?
Possible answers: I could get discouraged because the goal is unclear.

What happens if you do not have a clear picture of the product and your craft starts to look like you may have missed a step somewhere? How would your motivation be affected?
Possible answers: I wouldn't want to continue. I would become frustrated. I may decide to just give up.

How is having a clear picture of the goal of the Christian life encouraging when it comes to day-to-day living?
Even when you "miss a step somewhere," you still know what you are aiming for. You don't have to throw out the craft; you just have to keep pressing on toward the completed picture. Seeing what the outcome will be (and already is) makes the effort worthwhile.

26. Rather than judging a Christian who falls, what would be a better response toward him or her?
Encouraging the individual to experience what is actually true about him or her as a result of Christ

27. Understanding the goal is important in many aspects of life. For example, if you loved basketball and wanted to be the best basketball player you could possibly be, where would you look?

You would look to someone like Michael Jordan in order to master his technique, his skills, and his strategies.

Your American history teacher could tell you to prepare for your semester test by learning all information in your textbook and from your notes. But how might your attitude toward studying improve if, instead, she were to tell you which specific names, dates, and events to learn?
You would be more encouraged to study. Without knowing what specific information you are supposed to be learning, you can feel overwhelmed and decide it would be better not to study at all rather than to spend hours learning material that didn't even end up on the test.

What word could describe the natural response of someone who clearly understands what he or she is aiming for?
Possible answers: hope, encouragement, security, success, joy

28. Knowing you are already made righteous through Christ encourages you to live how?
It encourages you to live out what and who you already are.

DAY 5

 FOCUS

The Christian experience is living out the life of what is already true of us. God has made us partakers of His divine nature. Our godly living is not a result of our own efforts; it is a result of knowing God. God gives us many tools to enable us to put together the pieces of the puzzle that show what we are in Him, including worship, prayer, and His Word.

 **APPLICATION**

29. Indicate which of the following are accomplished by Christ rather than by your own efforts.
> a. your salvation
> b. access to God
> c. your standing as righteous before God
> d. the death and resurrection of Christ
> e. God's mercy
> f. God's grace

All we have and all we are is a result of who God is and what Christ accomplished. Nothing is a result of who we are or our own efforts.

When God has taken the initiative to grant us godliness according to His power, why do you think we so often take the burden to live out a godly life upon ourselves?
Possible answers: Because we don't truly understand the new life we have been given through Him and the facts of our standing before God. Because we don't really understand the extent of His grace.

30. Why is it so important to focus on God as not only the author but also the perfector of our faith?
Looking to ourselves and our own efforts to achieve godliness will result in failure. The more we try to muster up the ability to conquer a sin that we seem especially vulnerable to, the more frustrated we will become when we fail. We don't overcome sin through effort. We overcome it through abiding in Christ.

Which would be more beneficial—joining a self-help group that strives to enable its members to overcome their weaknesses or seeking to know God more intimately? Why?
We must seek to know God because it is only through Him and the power of His Holy Spirit that we are able to overcome our sin, not through our own efforts or through the efforts of anyone else.

32. Other than those listed, name some tools God gives us to enable us to put the pieces of the puzzle together in order to live up to what we are in Him.
Possible answers: prayer, praise, worship experiences, Christian written publications, the fellowship of believers, etc.

WEEK 3
A NEW ATTITUDE

DISCUSSION

Your attitude is your state of mind or feeling in regard to something. **What is your attitude toward something you enjoy?**
Possible answers: favorable, pleasant. I am full of anticipation. I do it willingly.

What attitude are you tempted to have in regard to something you don't like, don't enjoy, or even dread?
Possible answers: I may be very negative. I may be in a bad mood because of it. I'd probably be unenthusiastic.

What attitude do you have toward something you feel neutral about?
Possible answers: I'm not really affected by it emotionally. I put up with it. I don't give it a great deal of thought.

When you think about your own attitude regarding sin, do you find yourself desiring to participate in it, dreading the thought of participating in it, or having little feeling toward sin one way or the other?

Does your attitude vary according to the particular sin?

DAY 1

FOCUS

God hates all sin equally, while the world loves and seeks after sin. Those who love the Lord will share His attitude toward sin. Those who do not know the Lord will cling to sin.

APPLICATION

1. Violence, pride, deceitfulness, lying, and murder are all sins listed in these verses. Although the Lord hates every one of them, how do we sometimes tend to view particular sins in relation to each other?

We may tend to place sins on a continuum. For example, looking down on others is wrong, but we may not see that as being as "serious" as murdering someone. Telling a little white lie doesn't necessarily seem to us to be as bad as violence toward others. Yet all are sin; therefore God hates them all. His attitude regarding specific sins does not change according to "how bad" we think they are.

2. What do you think is the world's attitude toward righteous living?
Possible answers: That people striving to live a holy life should hold on to a few sins so they will at least be "normal." People who don't participate in sin are boring and a little strange. Ironically, worldly people may not trust those who avoid sin, as if they were "up to something."

3. What do you think it means to "mock at sin"?
People who mock at sin have the attitude that they won't get caught, that nothing bad will happen to them because of sin, that it's no big deal.

Can you give an example of someone who mocked at sin, only to find out the hard way the seriousness of its effects?
Possible answers: The famous athlete or movie star who "sleeps around" freely and then ends up HIV positive. The person who experiments with drugs and then ends up addicted, disabled, or dead. The person who participates in "minor" criminal activity for the fun of it, only to get caught and end up with a police record.

The Bible warns of the consequences of an irresponsible attitude toward sin. "Do not be deceived, God is not mocked; for whatever a man sows, this he will also reap. For the one who sows to his own flesh shall from the flesh reap corruption, but the one who sows to the Spirit shall from the Spirit reap eternal life" (Gal. 6:7-8).

4. The fool says in his heart, "There is no God." This doesn't necessarily mean mentally denying the existence of God. How do many people deny with their hearts that God exists?

The fool may believe there is a God and may even have accepted Christ, but he doesn't acknowledge God or allow God to influence him. He goes through life, day after day, void of Him.

5. Think of a time in your life when you were actively involved in sin in general or just enjoying a particular sin. During that time, what was your attitude toward God?

Possible answers: I avoided Him out of the fear of being punished I gave little regard to God's attitude toward my sin because the sin itself was more important to me. I felt "distanced" from God.

CONNER QUOTATION
Why do you think a non-Christian living a life of sin is less likely to see her sin than is a Christian who practices living righteously?

The person living a life of sin has had her spiritual vision darkened to the reality of it. The person who seeks to live as God desires will be open to what God has to reveal to her regarding the sin in her life. God reveals spiritual truths to those who seek after Him.

DAY 2

 FOCUS

We must not just avoid sin; we must actively seek good. We must not just reject sin; we must consider it to be repulsive. Avoiding some sins but entertaining others shows that our true desire is to "not sin very much" rather than not sin. We must give up those sins we embrace, abhor what is evil, and cling to what is good. As we continue to seek good, we will have less desire to sin, less tolerance for it, and more hatred for those things God detests.

 **APPLICATION**

8. Sometimes it may look as though certain sins are not crouching at your door. Maybe you are not tempted with partying, greed, or some other specific sin and you think to yourself, "I would never give in to those sins." How might this attitude actually make you vulnerable to these sins?

First Corinthians 10:12 says, "Therefore let him who thinks he stands take heed lest he fall." Sometimes

areas where we have experienced strength over sin actually become our greatest weakness because we trust in our own flesh to overcome them rather than the power of Christ in us.

HENRICHSEN QUOTATION
What is God's attitude toward those little pet sins we embrace, play with, and pet?

He considers them to be repulsive. They may not bother us, but they make Him sick.

10. What good has sin ever accomplished? What did it do to Jesus?

Sin nailed Jesus to the cross. Sin claims to bring about happiness, joy, and fulfillment. But in reality, it only brings about pain and destroys the lives of those who cling to it.

 LIFE SITUATION

Janiece was going through a rough time in her life. Her relationship with her best friend Gayle was shattered. Gayle had told some of their friends something that was very personal to Janiece—something she would share only with her very closest friend. Janiece was so hurt. She would never trust Gayle again and couldn't bring herself to forgive her. Then, Janiece decided to let Gayle know just how much it hurt. She allowed it to "slip" to Gayle's mother that she had skipped school one day last April in order to spend the day with her boyfriend. That would show Gayle what it was like to have a confidence betrayed.

Janiece gained a little satisfaction from her act, but she felt so lonely. She didn't have her best friend to talk to anymore. She didn't have her best friend to hang out with anymore. She felt like a part of herself was missing. She felt completely lost.

This is obviously a difficult time for Janiece. But can you see some sin in Janiece's life that could have led up to her troubles?

Janiece's own sin contributed a great deal to the problem. Her unforgiveness, pride, bitterness, and vengeance all made the situation much worse and contributed to Janiece's difficulties.

How could she have dealt with what Gayle did to her without giving in to sin herself?

She could have rejected her feelings of pride and forgiven Gayle—humbling herself and seeking to restore their relationship.

What do you think may have been the state of Janiece's relationship with God while she was going through such difficulties?
Likely, she felt distanced from God as well, not because God had distanced Himself from her but because she had chosen to follow a path of sin instead of following Him. When our own sin is at the root of our difficulties, our relationship with God will suffer.

Does this mean that we cannot seek God to help us in our times of trouble?
No. God is always receptive to us when we call upon Him.

SPROUL QUOTATION
If we, as Christians, are saying to the world that God is unforgiving, covetous, ruthless, bitter, and so forth because that is what we model, what are we saying His attitude is toward those sins?
We are saying that He accepts those sins—that He doesn't hate them at all.

11. Some sins are repulsive to nearly everyone: murder, rape, child abuse. But can you think of specific sins that are socially acceptable?
Possible answers: gossiping; putting down others verbally; driving recklessly; negative attitudes toward schoolwork, parental authority, and work responsibilities

What is God's attitude toward those socially acceptable sins?
He hates them.

DAY 3

 FOCUS
David was deeply grieved over his sin. We, too, should be grieved when we sin against God. Confessing our sin results not only in God's forgiveness but also in the renewal of our spirit and in a restored relationship with Him.

 APPLICATION
19. David could have kept silent about his sin. What excuses could he have used to relieve himself of the guilt of his sin?
Possible answers: No one knows, and there's no reason why anyone has to know. I am the king. People answer to me; I don't answer to them. I've never

done anything really wrong before. I've learned my lesson; I won't do it again. David could also have focused on everyone else's sin and judged them for it, serving to minimize the seriousness of his own.

Yet from whom could David never have kept his sin?
God

21. Why is it so important to confess sin that God already knows about?
The act of confession forces us to examine ourselves to discover what we are doing that is against God. Only after we acknowledge our sin to ourselves and before God can we ask forgiveness and commit to changing our behavior. Confession of sin is essential if we are to have a right relationship with God. He requires it of us.

DAY 4

 FOCUS
Satan deceives, distorts, and blinds a person to spiritual truth. Sin sets an unrepentant heart on an ever-increasing course of evil.

 APPLICATION
24. Why do the ungodly not fear God?
Possible answers: Because they don't know God. They don't acknowledge Him. They don't love Him. They are interested only in pleasing themselves and have no desire to know Him or please Him.

27. Those who listen to the voice of transgression believe they have control over the sin in their lives. They believe they can sin without penalty because they are invincible. They reason that it's their life and they have the right to get drunk or to be promiscuous if they want to. They think that they are in control, that they rule their sin. But what is actually true about their relationship to their sin?
They are actually slaves to it. Their sin is in control of their lives. It is master over them.

In the beginning, transgression doesn't speak...

Look at the last excuse to justify sin in the Student Edition: "If she doesn't lose her virginity to me, she'll just end up losing it to someone who doesn't really care about her." How is this statement an example of sin corrupting this person's judgment, blinding him to the truth?

Sin has deceived him. He sees himself as a hero if he gives in to his temptations. He is trying to turn something wrong into something that is good, thoughtful, selfless, and caring. He has been blinded to the truth of what God says is evil. He is also blinded to the fact that what he is doing is wrong.

31. What is wrong with the following attempts to justify sin?

a. "I have the right to do what I want to with my money. After all, I earned it."
Everything good in our lives has been given to us by God's grace. We have the right to do what is right with our money. We don't have the right to use it in sin.

b. "Why should I show my parents respect? They don't respect me."
God teaches us to honor our parents and to submit to authority. He doesn't tell us we have to respect them only if we feel that they show us respect as well.

c. "It's OK to copy answers from the textbook. Everybody does it."
The wrongs of others do not justify our own wrongs. We should be attempting to do what is right in the sight of God, whether anyone else is doing it or not.

d. "She may be dating the captain of the team, but I'm much prettier than she is."
We can't use pride in ourselves to overcome the sin of envying someone else.

DAY 5

 **FOCUS**

We must not deal lightly with sin. David was grieved to the point of tears over his own sin. The fact that he was so grieved indicates that he had been in the Lord's presence. God will reveal our sins to us when we fellowship with Him. Although we may be tempted to look favorably at our own "lack" of sin compared to others, God knows all of our sins; and they are all evil in His sight. If we confess our sins, He will forgive us and cleanse us from all unrighteousness.

 **APPLICATION**

37. You might not see yourself as being receptive to peer pressure. But how might you be negatively influenced by friends who actively practice sin, even if you don't participate in any of their "activities"?
It is easy to pick up language patterns, negative attitudes, and manner of speaking about others without even realizing it. It is also easy to develop a passive attitude toward sin when your friends' attitude toward sin is passive.

40. "Yes, I'm sorry I stole that CD from the music store. They almost pressed charges against me!"
"I wish I hadn't lost my temper with my mom. Because of our fight, I'm grounded Friday night and won't get to go to the concert."
"If I had it to do over, I wouldn't have cheated on the test. Ms. Grey gave me an F!"

All of the above speakers deeply regret their sin. Yet what is wrong with their "repentance"?
They do not seem to be as sorrowful about committing their sin as they are about getting caught. This is not true repentance.

What do you think is a good indication that someone is deeply grieved over his sin?
Being truly grieved over sin results in confession and deliberate steps to turn away from that sin in the future. If someone is sorrowful only because he got caught, he is likely to commit the sin again if he thinks he can get away with it.

43. Which is the best reason to confess and reject our specific sins?
a. so we will quit disappointing those who respect us
b. so we will quit disappointing ourselves
c. so we can feel good about ourselves
d. in order to avoid punishment
e. because we sin against God
The best and only reason to confess and reject sin is because we sin against God. We must seek to have a restored relationship with Him. And we cannot grow in our relationship with Him when we are denying the existence of or refusing to give up our sin.

WEEK 4
TEMPTATION

DAY 1

 FOCUS

God cannot be tempted by evil and does not tempt us to do wrong. We are carried away to sin by our own lusts. Giving in to temptation results in sin. Our will, therefore, must choose godliness.

 APPLICATION

3. We often blame others when we give in to temptation or make excuses for our weaknesses, such as claiming that circumstances are unfair. But where does this verse indicate the blame lies?
We are responsible when we give in to temptation. Friends may encourage us to sin, and circumstances may make sin possible; but we are the ones who choose to surrender to it.

7. Holiness, godliness, righteousness, purity, the will of God, and obedience are all examples of the ideal marriage for "the will." In the marriage of the will and godliness, what role must "the will" assume in the partnership?
The will must submit to its marriage partner: the will of God.

DAY 2

 FOCUS

Following Jesus' baptism, He spent 40 days in the wilderness. Satan chose this time to tempt Jesus. Satan's desire is that we serve him and reject God, and he tempts us in a similar way—when and where we are most vulnerable. Just as he tempted Jesus at the pinnacle of the temple, so he attacks the churches today. Just as Jesus used Scripture to stand strong against Satan's attempts, so we must know Scripture so we can use it as a defense in the face of temptation.

 APPLICATION

9. In this passage we observe many promises Satan made to Jesus. Do you think Satan can be trusted to keep his word?
No, Satan is a liar and the father of all lies (John 8:44).

Does sin seem to bring about the same unfulfilled promises? Can you think of some examples?
Yes. Premarital sex seems to promise intimacy, but actually brings forth guilt, emptiness, loneliness, etc. Lying to one's parents seems to promise freedom or secrecy, but actually brings forth a broken relationship, mistrust, etc. Gossip seems to give a sense of superiority over the one being talked about. It also seems to bring a sort of kinship among the other friends with whom one gossips. What gossip actually does is to call into question the credibility of the one who gossips, and it eventually makes him or her the object of gossip.

11. Temptation itself is not sin; it is merely the suggestion to sin. It may be subtle or it may come in the form of a very strong suggestion, sort of like a flashing neon sign. What is the step that always comes between temptation and sin?
The individual's choice is the step in between. If the right choice is made, sin is avoided.

12. When you have had a mountaintop experience in your spiritual life, what do you think is likely to happen?
Satan is likely to attack, tempting you into giving in to behavior or attitudes with which you struggle. He tempted Jesus immediately following His baptism, and he will tempt us when we feel closest to God as well.

16. We expect Satan to provide temptation at a keg party, in the back seat of a car, and even at school. But how is it advantageous for him to attack in the church?

We don't expect Satan's attacks in our own churches. Therefore our guard may be down, making us more vulnerable. We may not readily recognize his influences in the church.

18. What is the main purpose of memorizing Scripture?

To be able to apply it during times of temptation. The more we memorize, the more it will come to mind when we most need it in life.

DAY 3

 FOCUS

Jesus instructs us to keep watching and praying so that we will not enter into temptation. We must avoid environments and situations that create an atmosphere conducive to temptation. By avoiding temptation, we are not giving the devil an opportunity to cause us to sin. We must choose to follow Christ and His lordship in all situations.

 APPLICATION

21. What are some things that can help us avoid temptation?

Admitting that we are weak (John 15:5), prayer, making wise choices regarding where we hang out and with whom, Scripture memory, etc.

 LIFE SITUATION

Clay used to be offended by vulgar language. Cussing just irritated him. But then he met Cole, and they immediately struck up a friendship. They had many classes, school activities, and interests in common. Cole cussed occasionally; but Clay overlooked it because, well, other than that, Cole was a great guy. It didn't take long before Clay wasn't bothered by the cussing. In fact, he didn't even notice it. He surprised himself one day when he heard the same expletive come from his mouth that he had so often heard come from Cole's. At first he felt bad about it. But he knew that he was basically a good guy, even if he did let a cuss word slip. Now, he is cussing as much as Cole without giving it a second thought.

Deanna's church attendance was consistent for several months. But one Saturday night she stayed out late with her friends. She just couldn't make herself get out of bed the next morning. She felt bad about missing church; but after all, it was just one Sunday. She spent the next Saturday with a study group, and they stayed up late working on an important class project. Again, she was just too tired to get out of bed on Sunday morning. At least this time it was for a good reason. But now, she is sleeping in more and more on Sunday mornings and thinking about it less and less.

How are Clay and Deanna giving the devil an opportunity?

They are allowing him to get a foothold (a position usable as a base for further advance) in their lives by giving in to the temptation to compromise their standards. Clay gave the devil a foothold when he allowed himself to be around someone who cussed routinely. Deanna gave him a foothold when she gave in to her desire to sleep instead of go to church.

Ephesians 4:27 says, "and do not give the devil an opportunity." How does giving the devil one opportunity often lead to more and more sin?

Compromising leads to more compromising because our tolerance of sin increases. Over time, we can become almost "desensitized." And then the sin becomes routine. For example, a person may think, "It's okay to miss church this one time. God is not going to reject me for not going." It is true; our position in Christ does not change. We are not on a performance basis with God, but Satan can get a foothold through such rationalizations and it becomes easier and easier to miss church the next time, the time after that, and so on. This principle can be applied with any act of disobedience.

How could Clay have avoided the problem?

Clay could have explained to Cole that he really liked him but that he was bothered by cussing; then he could have helped Cole break the habit if he was willing. If Cole wasn't willing to stop cussing, Clay should have distanced himself from Cole, realizing there was a good reason cussing bothered him.

How could Deanna have avoided the problem?

She could have decided to be obedient to God and denied her desire to give in to the flesh on that first Sunday morning.

By separating yourself from situations, environments, and even people that can lead to sin, what are you avoiding?

You are avoiding the temptation in the first place. You are not giving the devil a foothold.

If you are dating someone seriously, are you more

likely to be sexually tempted when alone with the person or when with a group of people?
You are more tempted when you are alone together.

How can you avoid giving the devil a foothold in this situation?
You can avoid compromising situations, like being alone together in an atmosphere that is conducive to sexual sin.

DAY 4

 FOCUS

If we submit to God and draw near to Him, He will draw near to us. If we resist the devil, he will flee from us. We draw near to God through worship, prayer, Bible study, and choosing to obey Him and live righteously. Drawing near to God enables us to resist sin through the power of His Holy Spirit. If we are not submitting to His Lordship, then we are submitting to Satan.

APPLICATION
LIFE SITUATION

33. Franko's friend Pablo made a great discovery. He found the answer key to the upcoming biology test on the floor just outside Mrs. Draper's classroom.

"Come on, man," Pablo encouraged Franko. "I mean, I'm gonna copy these answers down and then get rid of the key, you know? It would be so easy! Let's do it. Nobody has to know."

Franko found himself quickly rationalizing to himself all of the reasons why he should go along with his friend. He wouldn't have to spend hours studying. He would have to memorize just a few answers. He was so bogged down in all of his classes. The stress was really starting to get to him. It would be so great just to get a break. And after all, why hadn't Mrs. Draper been more careful with that answer key? It was really her fault. She had no one to blame but herself.

"Well, man, are you gonna sit around and think about it all day or what? This is a gold mine! We'd be stupid not to do it!"

"It sure would make my life a lot easier," Franko sighed.

Explain Satan's tactic to influence Franko.
Satan put thoughts into Franko's mind that would justify wrong actions. He used Franko's friend Pablo to encourage him to sin. Satan tempted Franko at a time when he was vulnerable—when he was feeling stress from his course load.

The step between temptation and sin is the free will to choose. Franko seems to be leaning toward giving in to sin. What would be the best thing for Franko to do according to James 4:7?
He should resist the temptation, which would result in the devil fleeing from him instead of continuing to tempt him. Resisting the temptation to copy down the answers now means he would not have the means to cheat when it came time to take the test. In the long run, he will be glad that he didn't. Once Franko cheats, he will find it easier to cheat next time. Temporarily relieving his stress by cheating may mean he does not know vital information later when he needs it. If Franko's goal in life was to become a doctor, for instance, he might not know the foundational information to get into medical school.

34. How does discipline in those areas in which we can draw near to God keep us on the right path?
When tempted to compromise, we must choose to be obedient. When we are obedient, God opens our hearts to learn of Him. He honors our obedience.

LEWIS QUOTATION
How has God enabled us to resist temptation?
He has given us the Holy Spirit to fight temptation.

When you give in to temptation, how are you likely to feel later, when the appeal doesn't seem as great?
You are likely to feel defeated. If you draw close to God and resist temptation, through the Holy Spirit's power, you can overcome it.

39. What happens when we draw near to Him? What does He reveal?
He will make us more aware of our hidden sins—those we didn't even realize we were guilty of committing.

40. Have you ever heard someone say, "I'm not a goody-goody, but I don't do anything all that bad either"? This line of thinking assumes a middle ground—not submitting to God but not submitting to Satan either. If someone truly believes this, to whom is he or she submitting?
He or she is submitting to Satan. The devil would love

for us to believe that being a "regular" person and not committing any "bad" sins is good enough. This belief justifies sin.

DAY 5

 FOCUS

God is faithful to provide a way of escape in the midst of our temptation. But He does not force us to take it; He only provides the way. Although it is comforting to know that others have faced the same temptations as we have, we must guard against allowing Satan to use that fact to justify our sin. Jesus released us from the penalty of sin, and it is He who enables us to avoid giving in to temptation. The choice to sin or to escape is ours.

 APPLICATION

42. Sometimes in the midst of temptation, we don't readily recognize or respond to the way out that God has provided. Why is that?
Temptation is flashy, attractive, and loud. The way out may be gentle, subtle, and quiet. God does not force us to reject temptation. It is our choice.

43. Satan does not say to us, "If everyone seems to give in to it, why shouldn't you?" or "You're no worse than she is." What does he say instead?
Satan makes his thoughts very personal. They become our thoughts. He says, "If everyone seems to give in to it, why shouldn't I?" and "I'm no worse than she is."

Others have not only endured the same temptations we have but also done what in the face of them?
Others have rejected those same temptations. The greatest example of rejecting temptation is Christ, who faced all temptation without sin (Heb. 4:15).

44. What are examples of "trap doors" away from temptation and out of sin?
Possible answers: Scripture; prayer; a phone call to or from a friend

45. We will choose the escape that God provides only if we are choosing to do what in the first place?
We will choose the escape only if we are choosing to obey God. If we have no conviction regarding obedience, we are very unlikely to even look for the way of escape.

What will happen to those who do not choose to escape from their snare of sin?
They will die. The wages of sin is death (Rom. 6:23).

48. What does the act of flying away mean to a bird? What does the act of "flying away" in the face of temptation mean to us?
They both mean freedom.

WEEK 5
HOLINESS

DAY 1

FOCUS

We were created by God to be holy. He instructs us to be holy in both our inward and outward behavior, just as He is holy. Jesus provided the way for us to follow this command through the power of His Holy Spirit.

APPLICATION

2. Which of the following are examples of turning toward what is good? Which ones are examples of turning away from what is evil? Indicate with a "thumbs up" the ones that are turning toward good, and a "thumbs down," turning away from evil.

a. not going along with the crowd when they are speaking negatively about another person

b. separating yourself from people you know will influence you negatively

c. taking advantage of opportunities to tell others about Jesus

d. reaching out to befriend a person who is lonely

e. spending time alone with God in prayer, Bible study, and worship

f. choosing to avoid situations you know will cause you to be tempted

g. apologizing to someone who has wronged you

4. Would you desire to be holy if you were serving a God who was not holy? Explain.

No. If God were imperfect and possessed the same faults and weaknesses we possess, He would not be worthy of our worship. God is the key to holiness in our lives. He is the standard for holiness.

God expects holiness of all Christians. But how are His expectations for you unique?

God does not compare individuals in terms of behavior. Although humans may tend to think things like, "I'm not as bad as she is," God does not judge our behavior against the actions or motives of others. He expects holiness from the individual.

What should be our attitude toward the One who gave so much in order to pay our debt so that we might become holy?

Our attitude must be gratitude in the form of obedience to the One who gave so much.

DAY 2

FOCUS

Choosing happiness over holiness is choosing the temporal over the eternal. Our wholeness is a result of our holiness. The sun does not truly indwell buildings where it merely shines through the windows but instead indwells flowers which are given life through it. In the same way, God's Holy Spirit does not indwell buildings but rather indwells God's people. Because God is holy, having no evil in Him, He is worthy of a dwelling place that honors Him through a holy lifestyle. God protects the dwelling place of His Spirit.

APPLICATION

6. To be sanctified means to be set apart. From what are we to be set apart, if we are to live the lifestyle God expects of us?

We are to be set apart from the sin in the world. Though we live in the world, we must not become of the world, taking on its value system. We are set apart as God's chosen people, and the evidence of this is in our character and lifestyle.

LIFE SITUATION

7. Shanae says she is "in love" with Mike, and feels that she would be lost without him. Lately, Mike is pressuring her to prove her love and loyalty for him in a physical way. That way, he says, he will know she is committed to him. Shanae has evaluated her priorities. She knows that almost any girl would be only too happy to give him what he wants. But he has chosen her. The thought of him with someone else is almost too much for Shanae to bear. She is a

Christian, and she knows that sex before marriage is wrong. But this is the guy—the one she thinks she will end up marrying. She seems positive that God has chosen him for her.

What seems to be the priority for Shanae?
Preserving her relationship with Mike and therefore maintaining her happiness

What course of action do you think Shanae is likely to take?
She is likely to give in to her boyfriend. She has already thought through the reasons to justify her action.

If she decides to have sex with her boyfriend, what will she have compromised?
She will have compromised holiness. She will have disobeyed God's instructions regarding sex outside of marriage.

If Shanae turns down Mike and loses him because of this, what might she discover to be true over time?
She will be involved with other guys in meaningful relationships. So while she may have lost her happiness for a season, her choice to trust God made her whole. She would have honored God by refusing to compromise what she knew to be right.

8. What is the significance of the fact that the word happiness comes from the word happenings? How is this different from "wholeness"?
Happiness is a result of whatever is happening in a person's life. If the circumstances of your life are positive, you will likely be happy. If they are negative, you will likely be unhappy. "Wholeness" is contentment regardless of your situation.

As Christians, why must we always seek holiness over happiness?
We cannot be Christlike if we are not holy. Being Christlike does not necessarily mean we will be happy. In fact, happiness is often the result of compromise.

9. Although the sun might not shine inside the church building, how will the outside world know God (light) resides there?
The world will know by the "flowers" inside the building—the lives of Christians.

A building does not require sunlight, yet a flower must have sunlight in order to grow. How does this relate to our lives as the residing place of God's Holy Spirit?
As Christians, we require the presence of God's Holy Spirit in our lives in order to grow. Without Him, we are spiritually nonliving, just as a building itself possesses no life.

Imagine rows and rows of wild flowers that extend for miles. Some are smaller and have fewer petals. Others are larger and have more petals. Their colors vary from red to yellow to purple to blue in seemingly every possible hue. Each flower requires energy from the sun in order to grow, yet the energy one flower receives from the sun does not take away from the energy received by the other flowers. How does the indwelling of the sun in each of these flowers relate to the indwelling of the Holy Spirit in the lives of each Christian?
God has made each of us special. He fashioned each to be unique, yet all of us receive our life from Him. Just as each flower glorifies God because of the sunlight that casts its light over it, so we glorify God because of the Holy Spirit that sheds His light and dwells within us. The sun's life goes on within each flower. The light and life of the Holy Spirit lives in each life in which it dwells. And God's "energy" is never used up.

10. God is worthy of our holiness. What makes us worthy of His Holy Spirit's presence in our lives?
Christ in us. Nothing we have done or refrained from doing makes us worthy. Apart from His grace, we could never be worthy.

12. If you purchased land with your own money and therefore obtained the deed of ownership for it, who has the right to construct a building on that land? To plant crops on it? Have a picnic on it? Dig holes in it?
Only you have these rights.

The land could not refuse to allow you to plant crops on it. The land could not get up and walk away if you try to dig holes in it. How is this like our failure to give the Holy Spirit the deed of ownership for our lives?
God paid for our salvation through the blood of His Son. We are not our own. Our lives, and therefore our lifestyles, belong to Him. It is ridiculous for us to think that we have the rights when He owns the deed of sale.

DAY 3

 FOCUS

We learn what holiness looks like in a human being by examining the life of Jesus, the perfect embodiment of holiness. Jesus did not settle for what was good. He sought to do only what was holy, and He achieved this by doing only what God told Him to do.

 **APPLICATION**

17. If you possessed all knowledge for one hour, what might limit the good that could come to the world as a result of it?

The world's acceptance of what you had to contribute. If you could not get others to believe you had the answers or could not get support or commitment from them, you could not accomplish what you should be able to accomplish. Jesus met with resistance throughout His ministry on earth.

20. We may think we are doing right when we settle for what is good. Isn't that better than what everyone else settles for? Yet we must actually be satisfied only with that which is holy. Can you think of examples where settling for what is good clearly misses the mark of holiness?

Possible answers: Robin Hood wanted to take care of the needs of the poor; however, he stole from the rich in order to accomplish this seemingly noble undertaking. You want a good, honest Christian friend to win the election for class president so you spread negative, yet true, stories about her competitors. The accountant for a charity organization wants to increase available funds in order to help more people but uses illegal tax loopholes to achieve it.

24. What motivates you to seek holiness even though you know you are just a human being who will fail?

Possible answers: The fact that God expects Christians to be holy. Knowing that God is the One empowering us to live holy lives, that we aren't expected to achieve holiness through our own efforts.

25. Indicate by a show of hands which good things Jesus could have accomplished while on earth.

a. wiped out famine and worldwide hunger
b. overthrown all corrupt public officials
c. wiped out leprosy and other devastating diseases of His time
d. preached the Word of God throughout the entire inhabited world

Why did Jesus not accomplish these good things?

They were not a part of God's plan. God did not instruct Him to accomplish these tasks and therefore Jesus did not accomplish them. In reality, Jesus accomplished every good thing and fulfilled every need of mankind when He died on the cross enabling all to receive redemption.

DAY 4

 FOCUS

Holiness is something we must actively and diligently pursue. Holiness is more than refraining from doing evil. Some people are spiritually farsighted, being blinded to the needs of people around them. Others are spiritually nearsighted, neglecting the eternal in favor of earthly things. Keeping our eyes on Jesus is the only way to have spiritual vision that truly sees God.

 APPLICATION

29. What are examples of single words that would describe our endeavors as we pursue holiness?

Possible answers: diligence, perseverance, self-discipline, self-control

People who are spiritually farsighted...

Which of the following are indications that you may be spiritually farsighted?

a. arguing with a friend over theological differences of opinion
b. befriending a new student who has had difficulty meeting people
c. avoiding relatives you don't particularly like during holiday gatherings
d. never initiating a conversation with someone you don't know
e. neglecting your chores because you are too busy with school activities
f. helping a friend resolve a problem he or she is having when you would really rather be studying for the next day's test and completing other assignments

Answers: a, c, d, e indicate spiritual farsightedness.

34. If we are to pursue peace with everyone and avoid bitterness and discord, what characteristics will we have to integrate into our own personalities?

Possible answers: a humble attitude; the willingness to "give in;" positive, uplifting speech

When we are spiritually farsighted in our dealings with people, we cannot see God. Why is this?
God expects us to value people just as He values them.

35. How is spiritual nearsightedness a manifestation of the choice between happiness and holiness?
It is choosing the temporal (happiness) over the eternal (holiness).

DAY 5

 FOCUS

The Shunammite woman observed that Elisha was a holy man and prepared a room for him to stay in whenever he passed through Shunem. She saw that Elisha was a righteous man and was receptive to what God had to tell her about him. Because of her faith in the form of hospitality, God rewarded her by giving her a son. We must seek to live out the characteristics of a holy life: righteousness, godliness, faith, love, and gentleness daily.

 **APPLICATION**

37. How might we expect a prominent woman to respond to someone she really didn't know?
Possible answers: with aloofness; with suspicion; she might not notice him at all; with indifference; with an attitude of superiority

39. Why didn't the Shunammite woman respond to Elisha in this way?
Her response was a result of Elisha's lifestyle. She must have seen godliness in him and was, therefore, receptive to what God had to tell her.

42. Whose opinion are you likely to value more—the opinion of someone who has led a holy life and seeks after God or someone whose lifestyle is questionable and whose relationship with God is doubtful? Why?
The one who is in tune to what God has to say is the one who is trustworthy. The one who demonstrates a disregard for God and His commands will obviously not act according to God's directives.

44. What is the result when we are open and receptive to what God has to say to us in all aspects of our lives?
We will be rewarded with eternal rewards that can never perish.

WEEK 6
A LOVE FOR GOD'S WORD

 ## DISCUSSION

Think of someone you know well: your mom, your sister, your best friend, your grandfather. Briefly relate what type of reading material you would most likely see that person reading.

Possible answers: My mom would be reading a romance novel. My sister would be reading a clothing catalog. My best friend would be reading a sports magazine/teen magazine. My grandfather would be reading a fishing magazine.

Why do you associate a certain type of reading material with specific people?

Possible answers: We associate certain types of books, magazines, or catalogs with people based on what we have observed about them: either what we have seen them reading or what their interests indicate they would most likely choose to read.

As Christians, we should not only have an interest in reading the Bible but also truly love God's Word. Why is this especially true if our goal is to become Christlike?

We should love God's Word and hunger for it because the Bible is where we find out what Christ is like.

DAY 1

 ## FOCUS

The words of the Lord were a source of joy for the prophet Jeremiah and a delight to his heart. The Bible becomes a source of joy to those who read it, meditate on it, learn it, and apply it. It is only through studying God's Word that we hunger for it.

 ## APPLICATION

4. What are ways we can experience God's Word fully?

We experience God's Word when we not only read it but also meditate on it, memorize it, and apply it.

When we truly experience the Bible, what happens to our hunger for it?

We hunger for more of the same.

When we get into the habit of eating, for example, sweet things or drinking beverages daily, such as coffee or soft drinks, we often find that we desire them more. We crave them when we have done without them for any period of time. However, when we go on a diet or get out of the "habit" of eating or drinking specific things, what happens to our appetite for them?

In many cases, our appetite for them also decreases. We aren't used to having them any more so we don't desire them as much.

When you are studying the Bible regularly, you are more likely to hunger after God's Word. But just as is the case with certain foods and beverages, what is likely to happen if you refrain from experiencing God's Word for any length of time?

You are likely to find that your hunger for it is not as great. You won't hunger for it if you are not taking it in.

6. If a person reads a lot about sports, fashion, or world history, what do you think occupies a great deal of his or her thought life?

Sports, fashion, or world history

If a person chooses to read the Bible a lot, what do you think occupies his or her mind a great deal?

The Bible: Christ and Christlikeness; God's commands; spiritual truths

 ## LIFE SITUATION

7. Derek is a Christian, but Wendy isn't. Both Derek and Wendy own a Bible. Wendy's was given to her by her grandfather. Derek got his as a Christmas gift from his parents several years ago. Both Bibles have prominent positions on their respective shelves. Wendy hasn't ever really read her Bible, other than

the "In the beginning" part of Genesis. She would know where to find it if she ever decided to look through it, though. Derek, however, takes his Bible off of the shelf occasionally, mostly to take it to church when he remembers to grab it as he walks out the door. Derek hasn't really read much of his Bible either. But if he ever needs it, he always knows where it will be—right there on his top shelf.

Is there a difference between Derek's attitude toward his Bible and Wendy's attitude toward hers?
No. Neither Derek nor Wendy gets much use out of the Bible.

Why do you think there should be a difference between Derek's attitude and Wendy's attitude toward the Bible?
God's children should have a different attitude about the Bible than a non-Christian. Jeremiah's heart was inclined to love the Word of God because he was a man of God himself. Our love for God can be reflected in our love for His Word.

DAY 2

 **FOCUS**

God's commandments are not a burden to those who desire to become Christlike. Christians convey to others that His laws are burdensome when they disobey them and when their countenance reveals a lack of joy and peace. If we truly love God, we will follow His commandments.

 **APPLICATION**

10. Is it any easier for Christians to muster up the ability in their own strength to follow God's commandments than it is for non-Christians to "do right"?
No. It is impossible for anyone to follow God's commands in his or her own strength. It is only in allowing Jesus to live His life through us that His commands are not only possible to obey but a joy to obey.

12. When will the believer who desires holiness feel burdened by God's commands?
The believer will feel burdened when he or she gives in to sin.

15. God's will for our lives is that we glorify Him. We were created for that very purpose. When we disobey Him, we are getting off track in terms of His purpose

for us. During that period of time when we are living in disobedience to Him, we will be going through struggles and heartaches that God never intended for us. We will feel the great burden of guilt. In the end, we repent and are then able to fulfill His purpose in us. But we would have been able to avoid this burden if we had just obeyed Him in the first place. An example of this is the person who "experiments" casually with different kinds of drugs, only to become a desperate addict. Of course this person could recover and go on to glorify God in many ways, but there is a great deal of pain involved in drug addiction as well as a long road to recovery.

Can you think of other situations where straying from the path of righteousness becomes the real burden?

Another example could be the Christian who dates a non-Christian, living a life of rebellion. The Christian might not only give in to the pressure to compromise God's commands but also be committed to a relationship that lacks trust. The Christian could have spared himself or herself a great deal of pain both in terms of the relationship and the inevitable breakup if he or she had sought a Christian, someone who loved God more than him or her, in the first place.

When we stray from the path of God's laws, in whom are we putting our trust and what will be the inevitable result?
We are choosing to trust in ourselves. The result will be failure.

16. When you love someone, your desire is to honor, serve, and give of yourself to that person. If you claim to love someone but do not do those things, do you truly love that person?
No. You don't really love the person at all. Likewise, it is not possible to claim to love God and live a life of disobedience to Him.

DAY 3

 FOCUS

Without the Bible, we would have no hope of knowing God; and the world, governed by sin, would be in chaos. The Bible can renew and refresh, impart knowledge and understanding, and give joy to the heart. God's Word is perfect, righteous, and everlasting. For those who are obedient to its commands, there is great reward.

APPLICATION

18. How has the Bible had great impact even on those who do not believe in its authenticity? How has it even impacted other religions?
The Bible contains spiritual truths that mankind could not possibly have come up with on its own. Those who do not acknowledge the Bible have been impacted through the morality it has taught all of mankind and the Christlikeness that Christians have extended to the world. Other cults and religions commonly adapt many of the Bible's spiritual truths to their own belief systems, such as Jehovah's Witnesses, Mormons, Islam, etc.

19. Where should a follower of Christ turn to during times when she is weary with the stresses of life, discouraged by her lack of understanding, and drained by the world's influences?
The Christian must seek Him through His Word.

21. How are we assured that the words of the Lord are perfect, sure, everlasting, true, righteous, and pure?
We can be certain that these words describe the Word of God because they are also God's divine attributes. The words that describe the Bible are also words that describe God.

DEWOLF QUOTATION

Why is the Bible able to give us far more knowledge and understanding than anything else in written form?
The Bible gives us knowledge into spiritual, eternal truths. All other knowledge is temporary (1 Cor. 13:8).

DAY 4

FOCUS

The psalmist had such passion for God's commands that he cried out to God for help before dawn and meditated on God's Word at night. If spending time in God's Word is our priority, our thoughts during the day will be focused on Him.

APPLICATION

27. When you are away from home and missing your family, what could you receive that would "reconnect" you to them?
A letter from home

How is this like the Bible?
The Bible records God's words to us. It is His contact with us from His home, which is our eternal one.

28. After hearing God's Word, how do you think the psalmist would be brought closer to God?
By obeying His words

29. How are the objects that we reach for an indication of our priorities?
We reach for those things that are important to us. We reach for food if we are hungry. We reach for warm clothing if we are cold. We reach for others if we are in need of friendship. We reach for God's Word when we truly understand our need for it.

31. If the psalmist understood the meaning and significance of God's commandments, what would he also have great insight into?
He would know God intimately because He is the source of those words.

What might prevent a person from being drawn to someone who has great passion for God's Word?
Possible answers: intimidation, lack of understanding of the full depth and meaning of what God's Word provides, being a nonbeliever

35. The psalmist anticipated the night so that he could be finished with the responsibilities of the day and return to God's Word. For what purpose do we most often anticipate the night?
Possible answers: in order to rest after a hard day, to have free time to ourselves, to go out and have fun

If, instead, we anticipated returning to God's Word at night, what do you think our thoughts would focus on during the day?
They would focus on God and His commandments.

When the psalmist's days begin before dawn spending time alone with God, end with meditating on God's words, and are filled with thinking about them, dwelling on them, and applying them, what do you think is likely to be his impact on the world around him?
He will communicate his passion for God to others. The impact will be great.

DAY 5

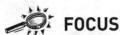 **FOCUS**

In order to determine if something you are told or read is trustworthy, you must consider its source. We know the Bible is trustworthy because God is trustworthy. It is the commands of His lips and the words of His mouth. The Bible is unique to all else in that it is part of eternity and in its words are life itself.

 **APPLICATION**

39. When someone tells you something someone else has said but then says, "Consider the source," what does that tell you about the original statement?
It negates it. "Consider the source" often means that the information isn't credible because of the person saying it, especially if the person is not trustworthy.

Who would you consider to be a trustworthy source of information?
Possible answers: your parent(s), close friends, people you have known for a long time, people who have proven themselves to be trustworthy in the past, God

40. What separates the Author of the Bible from William Shakespeare, Charles Dickens, C. S. Lewis, and Earnest Hemingway? Yet what is the commonality among all of these great writers?
The other great writers were all mere human beings; although their literary works still exist, they are dead.

Yet God still reigns on every word that is written in the Bible. What does this indicate about its author? What does it indicate about the Bible itself?
God is alive and lives on into eternity. His words are unique to all else because they are part of eternity. His Words have life in them: "The words that I have spoken to you are spirit and are life" (John 6:63).

42. Why is the Bible's counsel always trustworthy, regardless of the situations you face or your emotions that might tend to dictate otherwise?
The Bible is trustworthy because its Author is trustworthy.

44. Remember, Job lost every material possession he ever owned, in addition to his health and all of the members of his family other than his wife. In the midst of such immense loss, what was it that sustained him and provided for his very existence?
God's Word. It was his life source.

WEEK 7
RENEWING YOUR MIND

DISCUSSION

Why must a person renew a subscription, a prescription, a driver's license, or a library card?

Because they run out or expire. These things must be renewed periodically if we are to continue to use them. To "re-new" something is to make it "new" again.

What words come to mind when you think of the word "renew"?

Possible answers: restore, revive, extend, resume, continue, replenish, start over

Romans 12:2 instructs us to "renew our minds." What would cause our minds to need to be restored, replenished, revived, redone?

Thoughts focused on the flesh. Our patterns of thought must be programmed to follow another direction, a direction more consistent with the Spirit that is within us.

DAY 1

FOCUS

Becoming Christlike begins in the mind because sinful thoughts lead to sinful actions and pure thoughts lead to a life of purity. Conformity to the world keeps us from having a renewed mind and prevents us from understanding the will of God. Scripture memory and in-depth education into biblical truths are essential if we are to renew our minds to the things of the Spirit.

APPLICATION

2. What does it mean to "conform" to something?

Conform means to comply with some type of behavior, to be similar to others by acting in a manner that is consistent with common behavior.

How does a person "conform" to the world?

By behaving in a manner consistent with the flesh, a manner that is "worldly"; by valuing what the world values

5. How is the mind that is focused on worldly thoughts limited?

It does not have the capacity to know God's will—that which is good and acceptable and perfect.

7. How might we limit the Holy Spirit's ability to use the Bible to influence our thoughts?

By not studying it and not memorizing Scripture. If a particular verse is in our hearts, God can bring it to our minds so that we are able to use it. Our flesh would not "retrieve" the verse, but the Spirit within us can.

SPROUL QUOTATION

If our thoughts are more likely to center around a weekly television program, the calculus formulas we are learning in class, NFL statistics, or the latest edition of a teen magazine than they are to focus on Scripture and the things of God, what does this say about our education?

Our educational priorities are not in line with the spiritual education God desires for us.

DAY 2

FOCUS

Because as Christians we are in Christ, we are seated at the right hand of God. From this perspective, we realize that heavenly things have value and earthly cares are meaningless. Because our thought life is a matter of the will, we must set our thoughts on heavenly things. This is where our pursuit of Christlikeness begins. What we do on earth has significance only to the extent that it prepares us for or has an impact on eternity.

APPLICATION

11. Give examples of some things of heaven that we, as Christians, should be experiencing on earth.
Possible answers: glorifying God in our actions, praising God in our words, rejoicing with the angels when a sinner repents

LIFE SITUATION

Hershel found it hard to fight back the tears. He just lost the second grade spelling bee because he didn't know how to spell the word "absence." He always studied his spelling words. He always made 100's. Jessica hardly ever made 100's. She just won because her word was "answer." What an easy word! He could have gotten that blue ribbon. He could be the one up there on stage right now. He should be the one up there. He buried his head in his hands as he felt the tears rush down his cheeks.

Hershel felt very discouraged when the coach read off the names of "first-stringers" for Friday night's varsity game. His name wasn't one of them. He had worked so hard. His mind wandered back to the past few weeks. Things just hadn't been going his way. His classes were harder than he had counted on, and he found himself really struggling just to stay on top of his assignments. Juan and Craig didn't seem to want to hang out with him as much as they used to. He lost the Key Club election for president by just a few votes. What a disappointment his senior year was turning out to be! Why couldn't things just go his way for a change?

When Hershel was in second grade, what words describe how he felt after losing the spelling bee?
Possible answers: disappointed, jealous, sad, frustrated, devastated

When Hershel was walking off the football field after finding out he wouldn't be playing first string, how do you think he felt about losing the second grade spelling bee?
He wouldn't have even given it a thought. It would have been unimportant and meaningless.

When Hershel happily celebrates his tenth anniversary working for the same company as their senior computer systems analyst, how do you think he will feel about losing the Key Club election? How will he feel about losing the second grade spelling bee?

Likely, neither will hold any significance in his life. He won't be concerned about the election and probably won't even remember the spelling bee.

As Hershel moves through life, farther and farther away from that second grade spelling bee, its significance will fade until it no longer has any meaning to him. Even the "major" events in high school will seem trivial down the road. Just as time will take us farther and farther away from a given point in our past, when we see Jesus face to face, what do you think will be unimportant to us? What do you think will hold the most significance?
Worldly gain and struggles will be meaningless, while the spiritual aspects of our lives on earth will remain with us in eternity. Everything we do on earth has a purpose, but only to the extent that it relates to or prepares us for eternity.

16. If our thoughts of who we are in Christ are always in regard to the future, will we grow as a follower of Christ?
No. We will not be doing anything to further His kingdom on earth. Heaven will merely represent our future transformation rather than the transformation that we experience while we are still living on earth.

DAY 3

FOCUS

Although our own thoughts may seem harmless because no one else can read them, the Lord Himself understands every intent of our thoughts.

APPLICATION

The mind is always active...

How would you react if all your thoughts of the past 24 hours flashed on a screen for everyone to see?
Possible answers: I would be embarrassed. I would have a lot of explaining to to. I would need to apologize to some of my friends.

Why do you think we allow ourselves to have so many un-Christlike thoughts?
We allow so much sin into our thought lives because no one else can see it. There seems to be no accountability when it comes to our thoughts, while actions carry consequences.

Name some other beginnings to thoughts that bring about worldly scenarios.
Possible answers: "If I only had a...." "I'll show him. I'll...." "Wouldn't they all be sorry if...."

20. Why is it that the mind set on the flesh can never hope to have peace?
Only the mind set on the Spirit has life and peace (Rom. 8:6).

DAY 4

FOCUS

An impure and unbelieving heart is unable to discern right from wrong. An impure person will focus on the impurities in others, while a pure person will have compassion and see the potential that God can bring to fulfillment in the life of that person. Living a pure life is the best example of Christ for those who don't know Him.

APPLICATION

27. Why will the actions of one who is not pure deny God?
Because the thoughts of the one who is not pure deny God.

28. Consider two apple trees growing side by side. Both are the same size, and both have green leaves; yet one of them bears large, beautiful apples while the other yields small, shrunken, spotted ones. What does the appearance of the fruit tell you about the condition of the trees themselves?
The one that bears the good fruit has a healthy root system, and therefore the entire tree is healthy. The one that bears the diseased fruit has a diseased root system. The health of the trees is readily seen in the trees' fruit.

How can our response toward someone else's impurity be a reflection of our own purity?
When we see the potential of what Christ can bring about in someone else's life, this reflects purity in our own lives.

LIFE SITUATION

30. Arlene and Courtney noticed Rebekah in the hall talking to several football players. "Look at her," Arlene told her friend. "She's just flirting with them

so she'll be elected homecoming queen."

Courtney nodded in agreement. "Yeah, when homecoming is over, she'll shed half the makeup and find the time to make it back to our lunch table again."

Doug got a new sports car and with it, many new friends. Blane had never given Doug the time of day before, but recently he has been offering to let Doug keep his books in his locker, inviting him to lunch regularly, and even asking him to go to the stock car races on the weekends. Doug's best friend Jimmy was concerned.

"Can't you see that Blane is just using you because of your car?" Jimmy asked Doug.

"No, I think you're wrong, Jim," his friend said. "Blane has just become a good friend."

"How can you be so naive, man?" asked Jimmy.

Do Arlene and Courtney's comments reveal more about them or more about Rebekah? Explain.
The comments of the two girls regarding Rebekah actually reveal more about them than about Rebekah. In order for them to condemn Rebekah for her actions, whether this is justified or not, they would have to have impurities in their own lives, such as jealousy, condescension, and unkind thoughts.

Is Doug being naive when it comes to the recent attention he has been receiving from Blane? Explain.
Doug is not being naive; instead, he is assuming the best in his new friend Blane. He sees the potential in the friendship they have been developing. Hoping for the best in another person is not being "naive."

CHAMBERS QUOTATION
In the previous situations, is it wrong for Arlene and Courtney to not trust Rebekah or for Jimmy or Doug to not trust Blane?
Lack of trust is not wrong, but extending feelings of ill will toward Rebekah or Blane is. Being suspicious, being bitter, assuming the worst, and spreading gossip are all wrong. Arlene, Courtney, Jimmy, and Doug must look for the potential in Rebekah or Blane.

31. Explain the following statement: "When it comes to confronting the impurities in another person's life, actions speak louder than words."
Our tendency may be to point out the impurities in others, yet living a pure life ourselves is a demon-

stration of purity. When someone sees the purity in another person's life, it is the best confrontation for his or her own impurity.

Picture an enormous, pitch black room. Someone lights a match at the far end of the room. What happens to the light from that match? How can this be compared to the life of a Christian pursuing purity in a dark world?

Regardless of how big and dark the room is, the vast darkness is not able to overcome the tiny flicker of light. The light in a Christian exposes the darkness in others. It's not a Christian's word but his life that impacts others.

32. How is seeing the impurity in others an accountability issue for our thought life?

We can choose to see purity in others. We can't change others, but we do have control over our own thought life. The issue is one of lack of compassion/judgmentalism versus compassion/understanding the potential for what God can do in the life of the person.

DAY 5

 FOCUS

Wicked thoughts become lodged in our hearts when we allow them to give birth to sin. We must not only remove ourselves from the evil influences around us but also immerse ourselves in the things of God. Our choices in life regarding our conversations, leisure time, and friendships can either be supportive or detrimental to a godly life. Seeking the Lord's leadership in all aspects of our lives is the key to becoming pure in our thought lives.

 **APPLICATION**

34. What does James 1:15 indicate is the point at which wicked thoughts become fixed in the heart?

It is when we allow lust to give birth to sin.

36. What is the "soap" that cleanses our hearts? (Jeremiah 4:14)

Christ

What could serve as our "washcloth" and our "scrub brush?"

Possible answers: worship, Bible study, Scripture memory, prayer

39. If someone is more likely to dwell on the bad qualities in a person, how can he or she turn around this negative thinking pattern?

By determining to turn it around. By willfully focusing his or her thoughts on the good in others when thoughts of envy, bitterness, or anger creep into the mind. It can only be accomplished by allowing Christ to be in control of the person's thoughts.

41. When we focus on one object, what happens to our perception of the objects around it? How is this like our focus on God when we are participating in worldly activities and embracing worldly influences?

When we focus on one object, we see the objects nearby with our peripheral vision. We don't see the things in their entirety, and they are often out of focus. When we focus on worldly things, our thoughts cannot possibly be focused on God. We allow His influence to become out of focus.

WEEK 8
MOTIVES OF THE HEART

DAY 1

 ### FOCUS

Motives are the heart influences that govern the actions of a believer. We do not need to be concerned with the motives of others because the Lord judges their hearts, as well as ours, so that we might receive His praise. When our motives are to glorify Christ, we can be certain that they are pure. Any motive unrelated to God is not acceptable to Him.

APPLICATION

5. How does this fact relieve us from being concerned about what others think about our actions?
The opinions of others have no bearing on eternity. Only the condition of our heart matters.

7. In whose strength would our actions be carried out?
They would be a result of Christ's effort and strength, not our own.

8. If we find that we are concerned about the motives of those who are serving the Lord within the church body, what might this indicate about our own service?
It could indicate that our own motives are impure, stemming from the desire to please and gain acceptance from others (Titus 1:15).

BRIDGES QUOTATION
What words could we say when we pray that would serve as a "check" for our own motives?
Possible answers: "In the interest of Your kingdom, I pray"; "I consider all to be for the sake of your glory."; "For Your perfect will I pray"

DAY 2

 ### FOCUS

The correct motive for anything we do is to glorify God. Our motives have significance even in the small, routine areas of our lives. As Christians, all we do is a reflection of Christ. We must let this fact control our words and deeds. Doing all for the glory of God turns good deeds into godly ones.

 ### APPLICATION
18. What is the danger in performing a task in your own strength?
Deeds performed in the strength of the flesh cannot hope to fulfill the purpose for which God intended.

DAY 3

 ### FOCUS
The hypocrite seeks only to please others or advance his or her own interests when performing good deeds, having no desire to honor God through them. In this, there is no reward. Only words and deeds performed with pure motives behind them will be rewarded by God.

 ### APPLICATION
19. When we think of the word "hypocrite," what usually comes to mind?
We usually think of a person who professes to be a Christian but who lives a life contrary to Christianity—a life of sin rather than a life that reflects Christ. A hypocrite is a person who says one thing but does something else.

According to this passage, how can the most common definition of a hypocrite be expanded?
A hypocrite is not just someone whose actions contradict his or her words. It is also someone whose

motives for his or her seemingly good actions are wrong. It is expressing a belief or a feeling that one does not truly hold. It is insincerity.

20. Why does the hypocrite desire to be noticed by men?
Being noticed, esteemed, and praised by others helps the hypocrite feel good about himself or herself. People feel they have value when they are recognized in a positive way by others.

21. Even the best actions are not rewarded by God when the motives behind them are not pure. Below are actions that appear to be good. After the action, indicate an example of a motive that would prevent the Lord from rewarding it.

You sing words of praise to the Lord in your solo on Sunday morning.
You just want to show off your beautiful singing voice.
You invite a lost friend to church.
You're mad at your church friends and don't want to sit by yourself.
You spend extra time helping your dad with the yard work on Saturday morning.
You're just hoping to win some brownie points with him so he'll let you stay out an extra hour that night.
You attend a youth conference over the weekend.
You're going only because the guy/girl you like will be there and you're hoping he/she will ask you out.
You listen to your friend's problems and seek to give advice.
You just want to appear to be the one with "all the answers." Your ego is stroked because people come to you with their problems. It makes you feel good about yourself.

25. When do our intercessory prayer requests turn into gossip?
When we express concerns for people, not because we genuinely care about their circumstances but in order to feel "important" because we know something about someone else, this is gossip.

MCCLUNG QUOTATION
"Why did God allow such a tragedy to happen to me? I'm so careful about the things I do and don't do. I read the Bible, go to church, and all that stuff. I even invite my friends to go to church with me. I do so much more than a lot of my friends, and I don't do half of the bad things everyone else does. Why didn't this happen to someone who really deserved it?"

What does this statement reveal about the good acts of the speaker?
They obviously were not properly motivated. He or she didn't invite friends to church, read the Bible, and attend worship services in order to honor God. Rather, it is more likely that he or she did them in order to gain "favors" or "special treatment" from Him. In reality, we don't really want what we deserve. In our best moments, we are sinners and deserve death.

DAY 4

 **FOCUS**
Jesus called the Pharisees hypocrites because their outward actions appeared to be righteous, but their inward motives were evil. When believers allow evil thoughts to affect their actions, they are giving in to sin and the influence of the enemy. While people look at the outward appearance, God looks at the heart. We must live to glorify Him.

APPLICATION
34. Are we a product of the inside proceeding outward or the outside working inward? Explain.
Possible answers: What we are as a person—our attitudes, our expressions, our tone of voice when speaking to others—is a manifestation of the inward person. We are a product of the condition of our heart. All of our characteristics are a result of what is on the inside; they are not a result of what we wear, the color of our skin, the color of our hair or eyes, or any other manifestation of our outward appearance. Outward words and actions are a result of an inward condition.

People are naturally attracted to outward beauty. If you were to approach a person who not only possessed the physical attributes that you consider to be attractive (hair and eye color, a nice smile, a beautiful complexion, just the right body) but also was well-groomed, clean, and well-dressed, what would cause you to become "unattracted" to this person?
Losing your initial attraction would most likely be a result of the person's inward characteristics being manifested on the outside: words, attitudes, manners, values, beliefs.

36. What must be our response when Satan puts thoughts of jealousy, revenge, pride, or guilt into our minds?
We must take those thoughts captive: reject them

and cast them aside. We must focus on thoughts that are controlled by the Spirit (Phil. 4:8).

LIFE SITUATION

Estelle decided to befriend Natalie, a non-Christian. She pursued the friendship wholeheartedly, spending as much time at school with her as she could, helping her with homework assignments, inviting her to go to the mall with her, inviting her to church. Natalie, who wasn't that "close" to anyone else, welcomed the kindness Estelle showed her and treasured the relationship she now had with her new friend, Estelle.

Carter insisted on restoring the old car by himself. His father worked 60 hours a week and was exhausted at the end of every day. Carter didn't ask for his father's help on the project, even though he was a skilled mechanic. He didn't ask his neighbor to borrow any tools, and he didn't ask to borrow any money to buy parts. He used his own money that he earned at his after-school job, buying what he needed as he could afford it.

Did Estelle do a good thing or a bad thing in befriending Natalie?

It would appear that Estelle's friendship with Natalie was a relationship of great value, beneficial for both, especially Natalie.

Estelle pursued a friendship with Natalie out of spite for her best friend Kalani. Kalani had been spending more and more time with her boyfriend and less and less time with Estelle. Estelle became lonely and jealous. "I'll show her," she had thought. "I'll just start hanging around with Natalie all the time. Natalie would be happy to have a friend like me. I'll just blow Kalani off. Then, when Steve breaks up with her, she'll have nothing. I will have moved on."

Did Estelle do a good thing or a bad thing in befriending Natalie?

Estelle's seemingly good deed was brought about by evil motives and self-serving intentions. She didn't establish a relationship with a non-Christian in order to introduce her to Christ or even to help meet her need for a close friend. She did it only to hurt Kalani.

What do you think will happen when Kalani decides she wants to spend more time with Estelle, possibly even breaking up with Steve, and the two girls reconcile?

More than likely, Estelle will drop Natalie like a hot potato. Then the hurt on Natalie's part will be great.

Is Carter doing a good thing or a bad thing in restoring the car on his own?

It would appear that he is doing a good thing. Not asking his father for help seems to be an act of selflessness and consideration for his father's difficult circumstances. Because he is not borrowing tools or money from anyone, no one is being inconvenienced on his behalf. He is putting his wholehearted efforts into the project.

Carter's self-sufficiency in restoring the old car is motivated by pride and selfishness. "Dad thinks he knows everything about cars and I'm dumber than a doorknob when it comes to mechanics. I'll show him. I'll fix the whole thing on my own. Then he'll see that I'm really better at it than he is," Carter thought. And he sure didn't want to be obligated to anyone who helped him out in any way once the car was restored. He planned to sell it for a hefty profit, and he didn't want any "bleeding hearts" whining that he "owed" them for their contributions. No way. He would do the whole thing on his own, and reap all of the rewards for himself.

Is Carter doing a good thing or a bad thing in restoring the car on his own?

He is performing a task based on motives that aren't pure. His apparent noble actions in reality have no value.

What do you think will happen when Carter finishes restoring the car?

He may not be able to get much money out of it because his level of expertise was not sufficient for such a project. In fact, the car might not even run right.

How will Estelle and Carter be rewarded for their actions that, by all appearances, seem to be noble?

They won't be rewarded spiritually at all.

38. What do you think our complacency in the face of our own actions that are based on evil motives says about our concept of God?

If we think He isn't really interested in our motives or doesn't care about our motives or doesn't even know our motives, we obviously have an inaccurate concept of God's divine nature. We are limiting Him.

DAY 5

 **FOCUS**

Evil motives are behind our choice in friends when we seek out those we feel are "good enough" or those who can elevate our status, while at the same time rejecting those we feel superior to. If godliness is our goal, we must reject our evil motives and seek out those lightly esteemed by others. It is these whom God has chosen to be rich in His kingdom.

 **APPLICATION**

43. What is the irony in our trying to impress the rich while oppressing the poor?

The irony lies in the fact that those we try to impress by flattery or special treatment are the ones who treat us in the same manner we treat the poor, or those we view as inferior to us.

45. What is the reward in befriending those who can do us the most good? What is the reward in befriending those for whom we can do the most good?

We gain almost no reward in befriending someone for selfish reasons. We might briefly receive unreliable, superficial friendship from the person. The reward for befriending those for the purpose of doing good for them is eternal.

49. If we were to carefully consider those to whom we are tempted to feel superior, we might list the poor; the diseased; the homeless; the physically disabled; those who smell bad; the mentally handicapped; those who use bad grammar, bad language, have an accent; and the list goes on. If we take a look at our churches, we will likely find that few of these "inferior" people seem to occupy its pews. Why do you think this is the case?

It could be that those we are tempted to see as inferior get the message that they are inferior and are therefore unwelcome in our churches. Yet these are the very people Jesus called to follow Him, the very people He willingly served, the people He grieved for, and the people He died for. These are the people He welcomes into His church.

51. How does the birth and life of Christ on earth demonstrate the fact that He chose the poor in this world to be rich in faith and heirs of the kingdom?

Jesus could have been born into any social setting. He chose to be born and live out His earthly life in poverty.

WEEK 9
WHOLEHEARTEDNESS

DAY 1

 FOCUS

God desires that we seek Him wholeheartedly. We must never allow our emotions to dictate whether or not we approach God wholeheartedly but rather must obediently seek Him based on the facts of His presence. If we are to find Him, we must seek Him with all of our heart.

 APPLICATION

2. What would be characteristic of someone whose heart belonged completely to God?
Possible answers: obeying God's commands; making choices based on God's leadership; viewing His opinions as those that are most important

6. Why do you think our emotions are such easy prey for the enemy?
Emotions are unpredictable and can be very deceptive (just as Satan is deceptive). People tend to act according to their feelings. For example, if you have a crush on someone, you might act in ways that you normally wouldn't around that person.

How could Satan distort our "spiritual highs"?
Satan could deceive us into thinking our spiritual health depends on feelings. "If you're not experiencing a spiritual high," he might whisper, "your relationship with God must be lacking. He isn't there. He's not listening." In reality, our emotions don't present a true picture of our relationship with God at all.

7. Should we wait until we hunger for a deeper relationship with God before we actively and wholeheartedly pursue it?
No. When we wholeheartedly seek Him first, we will discover that we hunger for Him more. We cannot be satisfied to act based on emotions. Instead, we must act based on the facts.

8. In what specific ways may a person pursue God wholeheartedly?

Through Bible study, prayer, church attendance

LUCADO QUOTATION
If we attend church on a semi-regular basis, pray mostly when we have a specific need, and study our Bible when we don't have anything better to do, what can we expect in terms of our relationship with God? We may have all of God that we want, but we will not know the blessings that He longs to give us.

DAY 2

 FOCUS

As we approach our relationship with God wholeheartedly, He will create in us a wholeheartedness in other areas of our lives. The devotion that Jesus, Joshua, Paul, and Philemon had for the Father created in them a wholehearted approach in regard to teaching, work, self-sacrifice, and perseverance. In seeking the Lord wholeheartedly, we approach all aspects of our lives with the same commitment, working for the Lord rather than men.

 APPLICATION

11. What specific characteristics will we see in a person who imitates Christ?
Possible answers: selflessness, sexual purity, a witnessing lifestyle, service to others

We may tend to think of Christlikeness in terms of "big" or "important" aspects of behavior, but how is it also a matter of the attitude?
Jesus had a humble, kind, gentle attitude in regard to all things. Regardless of the situation, the obstacles, or the task at hand, Jesus did not grumble in His work but rather quietly attended to it with a wholehearted effort.

13. How does Jesus' death demonstrate our obligation to wholeheartedness in our relationship with Him?

Jesus demonstrated His wholehearted love for us by dying in our place, for our sins. Out of love for Him, we must wholeheartedly "die" to living for worldliness and fleshly desires that would hinder our relationship with Him.

14. Joshua was wholehearted in His obedience to God's messenger, Moses, and in so doing, he was being obedient to God. How is this same principle lived out in our own lives?
We must be attentive to the directions and instructions of godly people, those whom God has placed in our lives as representatives of Him.

18. When Christians work diligently to achieve goals without grumbling or arguing or even expecting praise or recognition for their efforts, who are they glorifying in their attitudes and actions?
Because this attitude is so contrary to the world's attitude, observing wholeheartedness causes both Christians and non-Christians to take notice, and Christ is glorified.

21. When everyone was discouraged and dejected, do you think Paul avoided them so they wouldn't hamper his enthusiasm?
When Paul worked on his tents, do you think he took shortcuts so he could devote more time to ministering to others?

25. How might our wholeheartedness to Christ impact the lives of others?
Others may see the impact Christ has made in our life and seek the same in their own lives. In that, He will be glorified.

SWINDOLL QUOTATION
How does wholeheartedness in our devotion to God transfer over to wholeheartedness in all aspects of day-to-day living?
If we are truly wholehearted in our desire to seek God, we will approach every aspect of daily life in terms of Him. All of our work and all of our efforts will be for Him and because of Him (Col. 3:23).

DAY 3

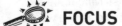 ### FOCUS
Wholehearted effort must be motivated by our love for God and our desire to do His will, never by the desire to please others or ourselves. The tasks we undertake, spiritual or secular, are worthy of our wholehearted effort, resulting in eternal rewards.

APPLICATION
37. What is the value in approaching even small, routine tasks, such as making your bed or setting the table, in a wholehearted manner?
The value lies in the return. God multiplies our efforts. Even small things are significant to Him. And our hearts experience joy in pleasing Him in the small things.

SPURGEON QUOTATION
Our society values some work more highly than other work. For instance, a neurosurgeon would probably be treated differently than a dogcatcher. The first-string quarterback is probably viewed differently than the "bench warmer," and the straight A student may command more respect than the student with learning disabilities. Yet why is their work of equal significance?
God does not view the value of work in terms of the amount of education it requires, how monetarily profitable it is, or how much it contributes to a team's winning record. He views the value of work in terms of the effort, the motives, and the attitude behind it. Wholeheartedly making hamburgers with a cheerful, willing spirit has much more value than begrudgingly or halfheartedly caring for the needs of hospital patients in intensive care.

39. People can be full of regrets during the course of their lives. One wishes she had pursued nursing school so she could do something she really enjoyed with her life instead of being caught in a dead-end job. Another regrets having held a grudge against a friend over a minor disagreement for so long that their relationship could never be the same. Still another wishes he had struggled through that difficult physics class instead of dropping it. Then his college physics course wouldn't be so difficult for him. What could have eliminated all of these regrets?
Pursuing something wholeheartedly—whether it be nursing school, a lasting friendship, or the course work in a difficult class—eliminates regret. "If only I had done things differently..." would not be an issue.

In what areas of your Christian walk might you need to be more wholehearted, therefore eliminating future regrets?
Possible answers: Scripture memory, witnessing, seeking God's will over my own, prayer

DAY 4

 FOCUS

Saul did not obey God wholeheartedly, and his half-hearted obedience led to his ruin. Saul desired instead to offer the Lord a sacrifice, but God is not pleased with sacrifice that replaces obedience. Halfhearted obedience is disobedience. Our wholehearted praying should be that God's will, and not our will, would be done in all things.

 APPLICATION

44. In verse 21, how did Saul try to make excuses for his disobedience?
He blamed the act of disobedience on "the people" and tried to put a religious slant on it by claiming they intended to sacrifice the choicest animals to the Lord.

How might we make similar excuses today?
We often blame our disobedience on the actions of others, such as: "I don't attend church regularly because of the hypocrites there." We may convince ourselves that our motives are pure when they really aren't, such as developing a friendship with a non-Christian who is a negative influence because we want to be popular but convince ourselves that our motive is winning him or her to Christ.

45. Saul probably felt pretty good about his accomplishments and his level of obedience. However, when God told him to do something he really didn't want to do, Saul decided to do something he would like better. But obedience to God is far more important than any sacrifice we could make. When God tells us to do something, He is specific. For instance, He might be working in your life on an area of weakness such as gossip. But if you are reluctant to give it up, what sacrifice might you be willing to make instead? Will God accept your sacrifice?
You might decide to give up secular music in favor of Christian music instead of rejecting gossip, but unless God has been dealing with you in that area, you are sacrificing in lieu of obeying. It is far better to obey in the first place than it is to do something God didn't ask of us. He will reject our sacrifice just as He rejected Saul's.

48. We may be tempted to be satisfied with halfhearted obedience, but what is the reality regarding it?
It is disobedience.

What could happen if instead of praying for God's will, you prayed...

for a boyfriend or girlfriend?
You could end up with a non-Christian who would cause you pain and sorrow.
for a new car?
You may discover all your free time being consumed with your after-school job so you can pay for it.
to win a class election?
You could end up with more stressful responsibilities than you bargained for.
that your mother would start treating you more like an adult?
She could make you start working part-time to save money for college.

DAY 5

 **FOCUS**

Hezekiah wholeheartedly devoted his reign as king of Judah to purifying the temple according to the law of Moses and ruling by what was good, right, and true before the Lord. We, too, must make our church participation a priority in our lives, approaching it with an attitude of willingness, gratitude, commitment, and a desire to grow in Christ.

APPLICATION

52. How were Hezekiah's priorities demonstrated through his wholeheartedness?
Instead of making the responsibilities of being king his priority and giving attention to the temple when convenient, he made the temple work his priority.

53. If you find yourself participating in so many church activities that your wholeheartedness is sacrificed, what might be a better alternative?
To pursue wholeheartedly only those activities into which God specifically draws you.

54. What are examples of ways you could be wholehearted in your efforts this week?
Possible answers: doing all class assignments thoroughly and with a good attitude; striving to be a wholehearted friend: treating others as you would desire to be treated and seeking out their needs rather than emphasizing your own; obeying and honoring your parents in your actions and words regardless of the situation

WEEK 10
HUMILITY

DAY 1

FOCUS

Although Jesus was God in human form, He lived a humble life on earth rather than a lofty one. Only through Jesus' humility to the point of death on the cross are we able to approach God. Just as God highly exalted His Son, so He honors and lifts up those who are humble.

APPLICATION

3. How will humble thoughts be demonstrated?
By humble actions

What other thoughts will exist in the mind of a humble person?
Possible answers: thoughts of Christ, thoughts of others, rejoicing in the successes of others

4. We sometimes view humility not only in terms of serving others but also in terms of not allowing others to serve us. Yet Christ, who was humble, allowed others to serve Him. He allowed Martha to cook for Him (Luke 10:40) and Mary to anoint His feet with oil (John 12:3). Salome, as well as many other women, tended to His needs (Mark 15:40-41). What level of humility must a person have in order to allow someone to serve him or her?
Not allowing others to serve us may seem to be an element of humility, but in reality it is an element of pride, the result of an independent spirit. Not allowing others to serve or help us may mean we think we are more capable or better able to do it ourself. Allowing others to serve acknowledges their abilities and gifts as well.

7. We wouldn't expect a humble person who doesn't seek attention to attract attention. After all, if we don't toot our own horn, no one is going to do it for us, right? But Jesus lived a life of humility, and it put Him in the spotlight. **Why do you think this was true?**
Possible answers: People were much better able to relate to Jesus in His lowly status as a carpenter's son than if He were born into a royal household. His humility drew people to Him and showed them what was important to God. The miracles He performed helped people understand there was something very special about Him.

DAY 2

FOCUS

The humble person willingly submits to a position beneath the hand of God. Humility manifests itself in concern for others, submission, and security in its own position in Christ. It rejoices in the successes of others. While pride attempts to draw attention to self, humility draws us to others.

APPLICATION

13. Is seeing yourself as too inferior to be under God's hand a sign of humility?
No. It is a sign of weak faith. We are under the hand of God because of His grace, not because of anything we did to earn that position. We need to recognize our relationship and position with God through Christ. He says we are His children, and therefore we are.

Why does being under the mighty hand of God result only in security and freedom?
He is our Creator and loves us unconditionally. The Lord knows everything and is in complete control. Therefore, we have the freedom to live our lives in the security of His power.

14. Which characteristics would describe a person unwilling to submit to a position under God's hand?
a. proud
b. halfheartedly committed to God

c. rebellious
d. content
e. independent
f. self-centered
g. seeks God's will
h. judgmental
i. flexible
j. obedient
k. devoted to prayer
(Answers: a, b, c, e, f, h)

LEWIS QUOTATION
How might pride manifest itself in the church?
Possible answers: unwillingness to submit to the authority of spiritual leaders, pride in personal spiritual gifts, "looking down on" non-Christians

 ## LIFE SITUATION
Victoria was really looking forward to going to the homecoming game with her friends in a couple of hours. She had just enough time to take a shower and get dressed, grab something to eat, wrap her friend Paula's birthday present, pick up Paula and Patrice, and get to the game.

"Vicki!" she heard her mother calling from downstairs. "Aren't you forgetting something?"

Victoria thought for a minute. Clothes, present, gas in the car. No, she hadn't forgotten anything.

"Danny has to be at Ricardo's house at 7:30," her mother said as she entered Victoria's room. "I've got to get this contract worked out for tomorrow's closing on the Cummings house, so you'll have to take him. And fold those clothes I have in the drier before you leave, OK?"

Victoria groaned. "Mom!" she complained. "Can't Ricky pick Danny up for once? I mean, I've got so much to do." Her mother was silent. "Why do I always have to be the one to help out? I have things to do, too!"

Her mother's only response was a disapproving look that said enough.

"I'm so sick of having to taxi that kid around...Fine! I should just expect it anyway. I swear I have to do everything around here!" Her mother continued to hear Victoria's complaints until her voice trailed off as she stormed down the stairs.

How do you usually respond to being inconvenienced?
Possible answers: by complaining, by arguing

How does your response expose pride in your life?
Responding negatively when inconvenienced says, "My plans are more important than yours. My life is more important than yours."

How does our pride in this area demonstrate the contrast between our value system and God's value system?
What we value is ourselves. God's value system, however, places the priority on the interests of others (Phil. 2:4).

How can we still be guilty of pride even when placing others' interests ahead of our own?
When our motives and thoughts are not pure: "I can't believe I'm having to do this" or "I'll inconvenience myself for a good friend but not for someone I don't like that much." When we are willing to put others' interests ahead of our own only on our own terms: "I'll help someone else when it's convenient for me."

18. **Why is humility not...**
...self-consciousness?
Humility doesn't spend time concerned about the "self"; it is concerned with others.
...despising arrogance in others?
That is judgmental, which is an element of pride. Also, the more arrogance you possess, the more you will see it in someone else.
...self-sufficient?
Humility receives all sufficiency from God.
...feeling inferior to others?
God values us to the extent that He was willing to give His life for us. We are all recipients of God's grace.

LEWIS QUOTATION
How does humility respond to the successes of others?
It rejoices in them.

DAY 3

 ## FOCUS
Paul humbly recognized himself as the least of all apostles, understanding that his sufficiency could be found only in God's grace. He viewed himself in the light of who God is. Although we may have gifts, tal-

ents, or attributes that would encourage pride, we must recognize that all we are and have has been given to us by God through His grace.

 ## APPLICATION

20. Why is it that all of us are the least of the apostles, the least of all saints, and the foremost sinners of all?
Because nothing we are and nothing we could do could change our status before God, which was freely given to us. We are worthy because of Christ.

21. Paul does not reveal an unhealthy self-image because he does not refer to himself as worthless or inferior. Instead, how is his self-image not only healthy but also a reflection of a teachable spirit?
Paul's self-image was not only a healthy one but also an accurate, realistic one. He saw himself in the light of who God is, taking no pride in his accomplishments or his rights by birth. Paul's boasting was only in who Christ was in him. Because of his humility, he was able to see that he had much to learn.

23. Where does pride place the credit for its efforts?
in itself

25. The humble person does not reject the compliments and appreciation of others for his or her efforts. Instead, what does the humble person do?
He or she simply says "thank you" or "you're welcome" outwardly, inwardly acknowledging the Source. Grandiose credit given to God can be evidence of hidden pride.

DAY 4

 ## FOCUS
God dwells in a high and holy place, yet He reaches down to lift up the humble. Our work for the Lord must be done in a spirit of humility, realizing that we could accomplish nothing without God's grace and blessing. No task is too lowly or insignificant when done in the name of the Lord for His glory. God rewards the humble with wisdom and honor.

 ## APPLICATION

30. An earthly king probably doesn't associate with peasants, other than his servants. Likewise, the very wealthy in our society are likely to have wealthy friends. Considering the position of the Lord, who might you expect Him to hang out with?
the important people, the spiritually superior, the cream of the crop when it comes to His creation

Why do you think God dwells instead with the lowly and contrite of spirit?
God seeks out the humble, those who have a clear understanding of their position in relation to Him. He does not seek out the proud who fail to see their own insufficiency and therefore His grace.

MACLAREN QUOTATION
What might cause us to think that specific jobs, whether in the secular world or in the church, are beneath us?
Possible answers: our educational level, economic status, spiritual knowledge

In reality, why is no job—either in the secular world or in the church—too menial for us?
No job is too lowly or too insignificant for us to perform when our motive is to glorify God.

37. We read in Proverbs 11:2, "When pride comes, then comes dishonor, but with the humble is wisdom." How does this verse go against the world's view of pride, humility, and wisdom?
People who are full of pride view themselves as wise and honorable. But the Bible tells us the truth: there is dishonor in pride. Only through being humble do we obtain godly wisdom.

DAY 5

 ## FOCUS
The Lord punished King Nebuchadnezzar for his pride by taking away his kingdom and banishing him to live with the beasts of the field in a state of insanity. Only when he humbled himself and repented of his sin were his kingdom and sanity restored. God reveals Himself to the humble. The rewards of humility are the honor and blessings of the Lord.

APPLICATION
GRIFFITHS QUOTATION
Which element of pride—race, class, intellect, denomination, spirituality, or subculture—do you think is the biggest barrier between Christian and non-Christian teenagers?
Possible answers: The pride of subcultures, or cliques; the pride of class

40. Do you think Daniel waved his spirituality like a banner and boasted about his insights?

No. Daniel allowed the Lord to honor him through his own humility. King Nebuchadnezzar saw the Spirit of God in Daniel, but it was not because Daniel proudly proclaimed his own abilities.

44. Nebuchadnezzar was proud not only of his heredity, wealth, and intelligence but also because he saw himself as what?

His words indicate that he saw himself with godlike powers and abilities.

46. Why do you think it took Nebuchadnezzar seven years to repent? Why didn't he repent immediately?

He was too proud. He had to first admit his own insufficiency before he could truly repent of his sin. It is likely that he first attempted to remedy the situation based on his own efforts and abilities.

49. Are there any rewards or benefits in looking down on someone because of his race, in despising someone because of her unspiritual behavior, in refusing to befriend a person because he is poor, or in disregarding the opinions of someone who isn't as smart as you consider yourself to be?

No. There are no rewards or benefits that come from pride. Only humility carries rewards.

WEEK 11
ENDURANCE

DISCUSSION

When you think of the word endurance, what words, phrases, or circumstances come to mind?
Possible answers: perseverance, stamina, running in a race, commitment, surviving, pushing the limit, coming out a winner, a test

Why do you think the ability to endure difficult or trying situations is so important?
Possible answers: If we give up, we won't know what could have been accomplished. Always taking the easy way out never leads to real learning or growing. Difficult and trying situations are a major part of life, so they have to be dealt with productively.

What are some ways our society reflects the attitude that if something isn't working or isn't going well, it's OK to just give up?
Possible answers: Over half of all marriages end in divorce. Children are abandoned by parents who become dissatisfied with child rearing or don't want the responsibility. People give up on a friendship because of a disagreement.

DAY 1

FOCUS

Endurance is the inner strength that enables us to persevere even when obstacles would encourage us to quit. It does not require immediate results, does not surrender in the midst of trials, and does not give up when forced to wait. Although we may not see the rewards at the moment, endurance for the Christian results in great reward.

APPLICATION

2. Do you think endurance is something that can be externally motivated?
People may be willing to endure certain situations solely because of a reward they will receive in the end, such as a wage for doing a day's work; but because endurance implies perseverance, it really must be motivated from within. Endurance holds to personal, internal convictions; and it is this which allows a person to accomplish things outwardly.

5. When Christians become weary because, for example, they are suffering persecution or they see the wicked around them prospering while them-selves are struggling or their prayers seem to go unanswered, in what are they placing their faith?
They are placing their faith in results, in the seen instead of the unseen. However, results that are seen are often temporary, while those that are unseen are eternal. (Heb. 11:6; 2 Cor. 4:16-18)

LIFE SITUATION

6. Alex is a Christian committed to his walk with the Lord. He's basically a content person but has been feeling discouraged lately. Several things have been going wrong in his life. Last week, Jenna was pro-moted to manager at their after-school job even though Alex works harder and has been there longer. Jenna even takes things from the storeroom. Alex wonders if she got the promotion because her uncle owns the place.

This week, Alex's parents bought his 16-year-old sis-ter a much nicer car than they got him when he turned 16. He doesn't see her as being any more deserving than he is. Today, he got his grade back for his semester test in chemistry, which he studied all week for: C-. Bud crammed the night before and copied some answers from Gail to get his B+. And then there's Hannah, a girl in the church youth group that Alex has liked for months. She won't go out with him because she likes Grey, who isn't nearly good enough for her. Alex treats Hannah right, and she won't give him the time of day.

"Maybe I should get a Harley and a six-pack and stop by her house some night," Alex thought. "Come to think of it, maybe I should move my desk over a little where I can see Gail's test paper better. What's the point in doing the right thing anyway?"

Why has Alex become weary in doing good?
He sees others around him being rewarded when they are doing what is wicked, while he seems to go unrewarded for doing what is right.

What kind of rewards are a promotion, a car, a good grade, and a girlfriend?
Earthly, temporal rewards. Years or even months down the road, those rewards aren't going to have the same meaning. Jesus said that the wicked will have their reward in full on earth.

How can we be motivated to persevere in our Christian walk when non-Christians who choose an obvious path of wickedness are the ones who win the election, get the recognition, or get the dates?
We obviously cannot be motivated in terms of the reward. Our motivation must come from within, knowing that God will reward us in His time.

7. Much of our Christian life is spent waiting, looking patiently toward the prize. What are examples of some things in your life for which you are waiting?
Possible answers: a much-needed job, a boyfriend/girlfriend, responses from colleges, a time when my parents and I can agree on things

How does Satan use those waiting periods to his advantage?
He may succeed in tempting us to be discouraged or to take an easier path. Therefore, enduring the waiting periods in our lives that do not seem to be producing much is as significant as enduring the trials.

8. God has the ability to give us what we desire without making us wait. Yet God knows the whole picture of what we need while we may only see a part of it. Reflecting on Isaiah 40:31, if we are rewarded immediately, what need might we have that would go unmet?
Those who wait for the Lord will gain new strength. If we aren't forced to wait, we might miss out on the strength that waiting would produce.

DAY 2

 FOCUS
Both a physical race and a spiritual race require commitment, effort, and overcoming weariness. Negative attitudes, laziness, displaced priorities, and poor friendship and dating choices slow us down in our spiritual race. Our focus must always be on Christ if we are to run the race with endurance. Jesus modeled endurance for us to the point of death on the cross; and as a result, God was glorified.

APPLICATION
Jeremiah 12:5 says, "If you have run with footmen and they have tired you out, then how can you compete with horses? If you fall down in a land of peace, how will you do in the thicket of the Jordan?"
How does this verse relate to our lives in terms of endurance?
If we have had a difficult time persevering in our Christian walk when the trials, difficulties, and discouragement have been minimal, how will we respond when the real obstacles come? Unfortunately, we are likely to fail in the midst of them.

10. In the midst of a lengthy, physical race, what does the runner do when...
...there is a pothole in the road?
He jumps over it or runs around it.
...she gets a leg cramp?
She rubs down the muscle and then continues the race.
...he becomes thirsty?
He reaches for the drink in his or her sports bottle.
...sweat starts running down her face?
She wipes it off with a towel.

What must we do in the middle of the spiritual race?
We must reach for those things that will help us endure: prayer, the encouragement of other believers, Bible study, worship

12. Do you think a runner would intentionally wear 20-pound ankle weights for the duration of a race? Would he go without eating for several days before the race? Would he stay up all night watching movies the night before the race?
No. A serious runner would make necessary preparations to finish the race successfully.

Why are our dating choices and friendship choices so crucial in terms of spiritual endurance?
People have a great deal of influence over us. The wrong friends or dates will more likely bring us down than we will bring them up.

If Christ is not our first priority, what will happen to the way we prioritize everything else in our lives?
Everything else will become distorted. Nothing will be placed in the proper perspective, and our lives will be chaotic.

13. We often think about how others hamper our efforts to run with endurance, but can you think of things in your own life which might hamper someone else in his or her spiritual race?
Possible answers: negative attitudes, inconsistency in terms of your own spiritual life, anger

Why is our lifestyle so important not only to us but also to others in terms of our spiritual race?
Our attitudes and actions don't just affect us; they also affect the people around us. We are accountable to God not only for our attitudes and actions but also for how they influence others.

19. If Jesus had not endured death on a cross, what would that mean in terms of our own endurance?
Our own endurance wouldn't be possible. His endurance made our endurance possible.

DAY 3

 FOCUS
God uses trials to produce endurance in the lives of believers. When we approach trials in an attitude of joy, God is able to teach us through them and give us the strength to persevere.

 **APPLICATION**
21. We wish it were possible to reach maturity in Christ without going through trials. But why is this not possible?
Possible answers: Trials force us to look toward the only One who has the strength, wisdom, and ability to deal with them. God uses difficult situations in order to develop our character. We can't learn patience, for example, unless our patience is tried. We can't learn strength unless we have first been weak. And we cannot be made complete in Christ without seeking Him, both in our difficulties and in times of joy.

22. Rejoicing in our trials means rising above our circumstances instead of grumbling our way through them. How does our joy enable God to achieve His desired result in our lives in the midst of trials?
When we approach our trials negatively, questioning God and possibly giving in to anger, bitterness, and other adverse emotions, we are not open to what God would have us learn through them. In fact, we are emotionally closed off to His influence. When we approach trials with an attitude of trust and joy, we allow Him to teach us in the midst of them. We are not asking, "Why me?" Instead, we are asking, "What does God have to teach me through this?" or "How can I grow as a result?" Joy lifts us above our trials.

23. How does God use our tribulations for the good of others?
After enduring tribulations, we are better able to minister to others who are suffering.

MCCLUNG QUOTATION
As Christians, we must understand that trials are part of God's plan for us. How does the world view God's role in our trials?
We must have done something wrong to deserve it. We're being punished.

DAY 4

 FOCUS
Endurance is crucial in terms of Bible study and discipleship. When God is not our priority, He will likely be neglected. God is the source of our endurance, that we may glorify Him. Jesus is the greatest example of endurance in relationships. When we neglect our relationship with Him, and when we give in to sin, He remains faithful. His life demonstrates that we, too, must endure in our relationships.

 **APPLICATION**
31. What insight does the Bible give us into God's perspective on a person's life?
God views a person's life from beginning to end. When we see from the Bible how the Lord worked through the trials of one of His people and the results over time, we understand that He was able to work good in the person's life in spite of bad circumstances. Joseph, for example, was sold into slavery by his brothers; but this horrible situation allowed him to become Pharaoh's prime minister and thus save his people from starvation (Gen. 37–45).

33. When will your own endurance in discipleship prove its worth?
"It is the one who has endured to the end who will be saved" (Matt. 10:22b).

PETERSON QUOTATION
What must we do in regard to our relationship with the Lord when we...
...are feeling depressed?
...start questioning why we are seeking God in the first place?
...become weary in doing good?
...feel distanced from Him?
...have been holding on to unconfessed sin?
...are discouraged, lonely, confused?
...are doubting our faith?
...are going through trials?
We must press on. We must endure.

DAY 5

 ## FOCUS
God responds to the persistent requests of His children by answering their prayers. Therefore, we must diligently make our requests known to God, that He might answer us in His time.

 ## APPLICATION
45. What are some wrong assumptions about why God answers our prayers?
Possible answers: our righteous living (we deserve it); our many words (arguing our point); our pure motives

What visual image does the word "seek" create?
searching diligently over a period of time

When we knock, why do we not merely strike the door with our knuckles one time?
The person might not hear us. When we knock, we strike the door several times.

Based on these passages, what is God's motivation for answering our prayers?
our persistence

46. What must we do when we become weary in our praying?
We must press on, continuing to pray. Our prayers may be answered because of our endurance.

WEEK 12
REDEEMING THE TIME

 ACTIVITY

Bring to the session several items which represent time—an alarm clock, a calendar, a stopwatch. Include an hourglass. Briefly discuss the significance of each in the area of time.

Which item best represents our lives on earth?
It could be said the only instrument that accurately depicts our life on earth is an hourglass. A clock keeps running, and 2:15 a.m. will come around again in 24 hours. A calendar depicts days, months, holidays, and seasons that will inevitably repeat. But an hourglass demonstrates the greatest truth surrounding our time on earth: We have only a certain amount of it in our lifetime; and just like the sand in an hourglass, once it runs out, it is gone forever.

What is the best way to make time your friend?
Possible answers: Use it productively. Use it wisely. Don't waste time or take it for granted.

Think of statements or phrases we use that include the word time.
I have some time to kill.
Time is money.
You're doing time.
My time is yours.
I don't have time.
These are the best of times.
time out
time zone
The time is at hand.
time and a half
She died before her time.
daylight saving time

What do these statements and phrases tell you about the significance of time?
We live by it. We are ruled by it. We are accountable to it and accountable for it. Our entire lives are a measure of the time allotted to each one of us.

How does a person's age affect his or her perspective on time?
Very young children have little or no concept of time. The perceived length of time varies according to the amount of time a person has experienced in life. Younger people see time as moving more slowly while older people see time as going by very quickly.

Does a person's perspective on time impact his or her time in general? Does it impact his or her use of time?
A person's perspective on time does not change the passing of it: whether an hour seems like 15 minutes or 3 hours does not change the fact that it is actually 60 minutes. However, a person's perspective on time will impact his or her use of it. A person who doesn't value it will spend it differently than will a person who views each moment as valuable.

DAY 1

 FOCUS

Our time is in God's hand, and all of the boundaries of our lives have been determined by Him. Jesus willingly submitted to the Lord's timing, and the psalmist derived security in God's control of it. The ultimate purpose of all time given to us on earth is to use it seeking God so that we may know Him.

APPLICATION

2. **What are your thoughts when you consider that your entire lifespan is in the hand of God?**
Possible answers: It makes me realize that He not only has control over the amount of time I've been given but also has a genuine purpose for that time. We are accountable to Him for our time.

4. **Think of something you would like to have, some activity you would like to do, or something that you need right now. How can you keep from feeling**

impatient, anxious, and concerned about having to wait for it?
Possible answers: We can remember that God's timing is best. We can feel secure knowing that the delay is because our time for it has not yet come.

6. Have you ever wondered what your life would have been like if you had lived...
...during the Civil War?
...in the Wild West?
...in a Communist country?
...in your grandparents' era?

Why were you born when you were?
God has placed you on earth at this time—in your home, school, town and with your family, relatives, friends—for a specific reason. You didn't live in another time because you were created for this time.

Think of a person who has had a great impact on your life. Share with the group what you think your life could have been like if you had never met that person.

God has given us the freedom to make choices in our lives. Why, if we are wise, will we want to be in His hand, under His control?
Only God has the power to work out every detail in our life. Although our choices may be bad, God has the ability to work them for good. He will have the final word.

DAY 2

 FOCUS

A wise person measures time in terms of days rather than years and strives to achieve goals daily. We should understand the brevity of our days and determine to use our time wisely and productively. With the passage of time comes death. Only the person who seeks God and prepares for a life of eternity with Him will leave his or her life on earth free of regrets.

 APPLICATION

8. No one can deny the importance of having long-range goals: a profession you would like to be a part of in 10 years, marriage to someone you love, children. But what would be the impact if, for example, instead of determining to lose 20 pounds by summer, you decided to eat right and exercise today? And what if you made that your goal every day?

Each day would represent accomplishment. And when there is accomplishment in each day, there is great success in each month and year.

 LIFE SITUATION

Janie is five years old. She loves to play dress-up. She puts on her play makeup every morning; walks around in her mother's high-heeled shoes; and helps her mother cook, set the table, and fold the clothes. She considers going outside to play with her friends but decides that climbing trees isn't ladylike. She would like to watch cartoons, but daytime dramas and talk shows are much more grown-up. She thinks it would be fun to have a tricycle, but tricycles are really just for babies. And Janie is not a baby. She is all grown up.

What is Janie missing out on?
She's missing out on the fun of being a child because she's too anxious to rush into adulthood.

How might we be guilty of the same thing?
When we are more concerned with our own timing than with God's and we act on it, we are in danger of missing out on what we've already been given just so we can rush into the experience we want.

15. What about the way a person has lived his or her life do you think will make him or her most likely to die without regrets?
The only thing that will enable a person to die without regrets is if he or she has lived a life that has prepared him or her for eternity with God, has placed the greatest value on eternal things, and has strived to obey His commands and grow in Christlikeness. In this, there can be no regrets.

DAY 3

 FOCUS

Each moment is significant in the Christian walk because it either brings you closer to life in Him or it brings you closer to death. Anything contrary to Christ and Christlikeness must be avoided. We are wise to seek the Lord's will in our lives and can do so through prayer, Bible study, living a holy life, and assembling with believers. In doing those things we already know to be His will, we are likely to discover His will for our lives.

APPLICATION

TOZER QUOTATION

How can it be possible for a Christian to attend Sunday School every Sunday morning for 20 years and still have little knowledge and understanding of God and a shallow relationship with Him?

We do not know God as a result of one hour of obedience per week. The key to knowing Him is devoting time to Him.

24. What is the likely result of watching sit coms and dramas on TV for three hours during the evening? What will you take away from the experience?

You will take away very little, if anything. The experience will have little bearing on your life the next day, and you are likely to have forgotten what the programs were about within a week or two.

What is the likely result of studying the Bible, praying, and seeking God and His direction in your life? What will you take away from the experience?

The result will inevitably be a deeper relationship with Him, a greater knowledge and understanding of Him, and a greater sense of direction and His will in your life.

DAY 4

FOCUS

God has delayed His return for a purpose. He is patient, desiring that all should be saved. We must view our time on earth as an opportunity to impact the kingdom of God through witnessing to the lost. Failing to use our time to seek Him will leave us vulnerable to worldliness and distorted teaching.

APPLICATION

25. How does God view your past, present, and future, birth to death?

He views them not in terms of time, or the progression of time, but rather in one glimpse. While we may be slaves to it, God is not bound in any way by time.

How does this give you confidence?

In placing our lives in His hand, we are giving control to the Creator who knows all and controls all.

27. Considering the fact that God has not yet returned because of the lost, how should that spur us on to action?

We must look at time as an opportunity to witness to the lost. He has delayed His return for a reason: so we can share Christ with those who otherwise will perish.

28. How does verse 13 encourage you in your Christian walk on earth?

Although we must struggle in a world where wickedness reigns, we are headed toward a new earth where righteousness dwells. We will no longer be struggling to be righteous in an unrighteous world; we will be joyously experiencing righteousness in a righteous world.

31. Complete the following sentences with the first word that comes to mind:
Devoting our time to seeking God results in

_____.
Possible answers: peace, security, wisdom, knowledge, understanding, joy, growth, stability
Being satisfied with a shallow, uncommitted relationship with God results in _____.
Possible answers: struggles, confusion, frustration, uncertainty, unrighteousness, void, inconsistency

LUCADO QUOTATION

What other emotions such as self-pity, anxiety, and boredom do you think contaminate the time you have on earth?
Possible answers: anger, bitterness, selfishness, laziness, holding grudges

DAY 5

FOCUS

We can learn a great deal from the ant, who works diligently even in the absence of leadership. Laziness is a sin which leads to poverty. We must, instead, be diligent and fervent in our work, that we might share with those in need. Any task we perform can be used as a tool when done with energy and cheerfulness.

APPLICATION

35. An ant can often be seen carrying a piece of food that is much larger and heavier than the ant itself. What can we learn from this?

We can learn persistence and endurance.

Ants don't just "do their own thing." We never see an ant hiding and hoarding a tidbit for its own use. Instead, ants are always seen working together.

What can we learn from this?
We can learn dependence and teamwork.

Ants will even link up over a puddle of water to make a bridge with their bodies so that other ants can carry food across the water to the anthill. What can we learn from this?
Ants will do whatever work needs to be done, no matter how "lowly" a particular task might be. The "menial" jobs add up to success.

38. Time is either a tool or a couch as related to a task. What determines its use?
Possible answers: the attitude of the user, their level of motivation

WEEK 13
SELF-CONTROL

DAY 1

 FOCUS

Self-control is identified as a fruit of the Spirit in Galatians 5:22-23. Because we are Christians, we are capable of self-control; but we must cultivate it in our lives in order to experience it. Our adequacy in all areas comes, not from ourselves, but from God. Because of who we are in Christ, self-control is actually God's control.

 APPLICATION

Proverbs 17:27 says, "He who restrains his words has knowledge, and he who has a cool spirit is a man of understanding." How does this verse contrast the methods by which people often attempt to display their knowledge?
People often try to demonstrate their wisdom through persistently arguing a point. But according to this verse, the person who demonstrates this lack of control in words and actions actually lacks wisdom.

1. People try to experience joy and peace in their lives in many ways, but they do not go to the Source of joy and peace. In what ways might people try to obtain it?
Possible answers: by using drugs, in sexual relationships, by immersing themselves in a cause

In what way might these things be considered anti-Christs?
They all claim to produce in a person the things that only the Holy Spirit can produce.

KELLER QUOTATION
Why do you think God puts us in situations where we are not able to have self control?
In this way, we will see that we cannot have self-control on our own; we must turn to God. The kind of self-control that pleases God is the kind of which He is the source (John 15:5).

DAY 2

 FOCUS

A person who lacks self-control leaves himself vulnerable to the attacks of the enemy. The lack of self-control results in the deeds of the flesh, while the control of the Spirit results in the fruit of the Spirit. While the world may view wit and physical domination as indications of strength, real strength lies in the ability to control the inner person. Self-control is the ability to not only control words and actions but also emotions.

 APPLICATION

7. Indicate one-word answers that would describe a person who goes to bed without locking (or even closing) windows and doors first.
Possible answers: vulnerable, defenseless, unwise, unprepared

If a person is unable to control herself, how do you think she will be able to control the effect others' words and actions have on her? In other words, if you find it difficult to control your temper when you wake up in a bad mood, how do you think you will respond when others "rub you the wrong way"?
If you do not have self-control when it comes to yourself, you will be unable to control the effect others have on you. If you can't control a bad mood, you won't be able to keep from becoming angry when someone frustrates you. You have left the doors and windows of your emotions unlocked and are therefore vulnerable, defenseless, unwise, and unprepared.

8. In contrast to the fruit of the Spirit, spelled out in verses 22-23, what might the deeds of the flesh be considered?
They are the fruits of the flesh.

✦ LIFE SITUATION

Sandy started to turn the corner in the hall at school until she heard familiar voices mentioning her name. She leaned against the wall and listened.

"Well, if you ask me, the only reason Parker asked her out is because she flirts with him, like, all the time. He probably thinks she's easy or something." That was Jan, who Sandy had considered to be her best friend.

"Well, I think we should teach her a lesson," Sandy heard Jayce's voice this time. "I mean, why should we just go around acting like everything's OK and all, when Sandy knows Shaunna has had a crush on him for, you know, the whole year? I think Sandy should just find somebody else."

"Yeah," the others agreed.

"So what do you think we should do?" asked Casie.

"I think we should just blow her off," said Jan. "You know, let her know we think what she's doing stinks. She's supposed to meet us here for lunch, right?" The others nodded. "So, let's just not show up. Casie, let's meet at your locker instead. We'll be gone before she even realizes she's been stood up!" The other girls laughed as Sandy darted into the nearby rest room, her eyes beginning to fill with tears.

DISCUSSION

What specific deeds of the flesh are these girls guilty of committing?
Possible answers: Enmity, strife, jealousy, disputes, dissensions, factions. They are talking negatively about someone else and plotting against her with the sole purpose of inflicting emotional pain upon her.

What kind of self-control are these girls showing?
They are not demonstrating self-control in their thoughts or actions. They are letting their emotions control their words and behavior. And their lack of self-control has left them vulnerable to the influences of the enemy.

How do you think the girls might attempt to justify their actions? Would they be right?
Sandy deserves it. She's brought it on herself by not considering Shaunna's feelings and by behaving in a way that is not acceptable to them. Of course they would not be right in their actions because they do not have the right to condemn Sandy.

Casie, for example, might not have had any ill feelings toward Sandy before this conversation took place. How do you think she will now feel, as a result of the girls' lack of self-control in their discussion?
Now Casie is likely to feel the same way about Sandy and her actions toward Parker as the other girls do. Gossip can lead to hate, even when there was none to begin with.

If the girls had closed their doors to the enemy and allowed the influence of the Spirit to take control, what might have been their response to Sandy?
They would not have been talking about her. They would have approached her actions with an attitude of love and acceptance and treated her with gentleness, patience, and kindness.

If one of the girls decides to do the right thing and meet Sandy for lunch, do you think the problem will be resolved?
No. The other girls will be angry with her. She will be forced to take a side. Doing the right thing after failing to exercise self-control does not always heal all of the wounds. The inability to control oneself can have long-term effects.

9. If the girls in the above life situation had used self-control, what would have been avoided?
They may have been tempted to talk bad about Sandy, or at least to go along with those who did; but if they had used self-control and refused to insult her, then Sandy's feelings would not have been hurt.

How might the Holy Spirit warn you when you are about to lose control in the area of, for example, gossiping?
When you find yourself prefacing something you are about to tell someone with the words, "I really shouldn't tell you this, but..." it is probably the Holy Spirit warning you.

What does Satan say when the Spirit warns you?
Possible answers: "This won't hurt." "It's only one person you're telling." "You can trust him."

What steps can we take to ensure that the doors and windows in our lives are locked to the influences of the enemy?
Possible answers: Meet with God in prayer and Bible study daily. Fellowship with godly people.

12. Two guys who are the same size find themselves disagreeing over something they consider to be very important. Words lead to anger, and anger leads to rage. Soon one is challenging the other to a fight after school. Who will be considered the strongest?
The one who wins the physical fight

Who would be the one with real strength?
The one who controlled his temper and refused to fight would be the one with real strength.

13. What will always avoid when you use self-control in the first place?
Regret

15. What do you think is the first step in controlling our emotions?
The first step is controlling our thought life. If we reject thoughts that result in specific emotions, we can control them.

MACLAREN QUOTATION
What are examples of emotions worth cultivating? Which must we repress?
Cultivate love, peace, patience, acceptance. Repress hatred, bitterness, jealousy, anger.

DAY 3

FOCUS
We must put limitations on almost every aspect of our lives because too much of anything can lead to disaster. The greatest opposition in a Christian's spiritual race is within his own body. We must make our bodies our slaves, giving control to God because our adequacy is from Him. In so doing, we will finish the race and receive the imperishable wreath.

APPLICATION
16. When we refuse to set limits in the areas mentioned in question 16, why are we guilty of the most extreme form of self-centeredness?
When we do not control our impulses and set limits on our actions, we are doing so because we feel that our happiness, our satisfaction, our feelings are more important than anything or anyone else.

Work can be a subtle enemy because we view it as something good. When does it become bad?
When it controls us, just as anything that controls us is bad.

22. When we rely on ourselves to give control to God and to live in obedience to Him, what will happen?
We will fail. We will give Him control only to take it back later.

24. If you drove away in a car without any predetermined destination, the following could happen:
a. You could run out of gas and stall.
b. You could get completely lost.
c. You could end up with car problems and there would be no one to help you.
d. You could damage your reputation as a logical-thinking person.

What comparisons could you make with the above statements and Christians who run a race without aim or merely beat the air?
Possible answers:
a. They could lose the drive that motivated them in the first place. Because they are controlled by their emotions, when the spiritual high wears off, they will fall away.
b. They could lose sight of the prize and seek other means to fulfill temporal needs.
c. When they run into difficulties in life and are forced to go through trials, they could unsuccessfully seek means other than God to rescue them.
d. They could damage their witness because of their inconsistency and lack of commitment.

DAY 4

FOCUS
Anger is something in our lives that we must control because it, like other sins, is a matter of choice. Instead of letting the anger of others bring our own anger to the surface, we must respond with gentleness and composure. We must exercise self-control in our use of time as well as over forms of self-gratification.

APPLICATION
27. When we have a close friend involved in drugs, alcohol, or any other vice resulting from a lack of self-control, we may try to convince ourselves that we can rescue him from the problem. But why is this not possible?
We cannot rescue another person. The person must rely on God alone to rescue him. We are helpless to rescue ourself from trouble; therefore, how is it conceivable that we could rescue someone else?

What, then, do we have to offer in relationships?
The only thing we have to offer others in our relationships with them is Christ.

28. All sin is addictive. Describe the cycle that begins once a particular sin is committed for the first time.
The first time you give in to it, there will probably be a measure of guilt involved. The second time you are tempted, it will be a little bit easier to give in to it. After a while, you may no longer see it as sin. You may even reach the point where you don't care whether it is sin or not.

BACKUS/CHAPIAN QUOTATION
How is anger often a form of self-centeredness?
We often become angry when someone offends us or we are inconvenienced or someone disagrees with our point of view. We become angry with anything that interferes with our lives or threatens our authority. Anger is a defense mechanism in which we fight for that which is our priority—ourselves.

32. According to Proverbs 13:20: "He who walks with wise men will be wise, but the companion of fools will suffer harm." When you associate with people your parents consider a negative influence, what kinds of things might you pick up from them?
Possible answers: their lingo; their bad habits including addictions; their way of looking at things, such as negativism

36. Our countenance is an area of self-control that we often overlook. "I feel depressed, so I have to be in a bad mood." How might we excuse giving in to such emotions?
We may justify an unpleasant disposition or bad mood by thinking we don't want to be fake. We reason that others just have to accept us the way we are.

When we give in to a bad mood, we are letting our emotions control us. Instead, what must we choose?
We must choose to be holy in every way, whether our emotions dictate holiness to us or not.

38. In our busy lives with our seemingly impossible schedules, we may consider ourselves to be slaves to time. Instead, how should we view our time?
As something we control. Our time should be in subjection to us and what we know to be important.

DAY 5

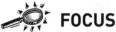 **FOCUS**
In Genesis we read of Jacob and Leah's daughter, Dinah, who was raped by Shechem. As a result of his lack of self-control, he and many others lost their lives. Lacking self-control can have devastating effects not only on those involved but also on many others. Love and self-control cannot be separated. Because love is patient, it will always lead to what is proper.

APPLICATION
51. How could Dinah have avoided this disaster?
She was alone in a foreign land for unknown reasons. She could have avoided trouble by being with her people where she was supposed to be.

What would have been the impact if Shechem had exercised self-control?
If he had controlled himself until the desire passed, his entire village, as well as his own life, would have been spared.

What emotion played on the brothers and caused them to act so brutally?
Anger

52. The emotion of love Shechem claimed for Dinah was inconsistent with his initial actions toward her. Is it possible to separate love from self-control?
No. If a person really loves someone, self-control will be a part of the relationship.

53. What would be your reaction if you heard the words, "If you love me, you will turn me on, sexually"?
Lust is not love, and the person giving in to lust lacks self-control. The person who utters these words is not looking out for the interests of the other person but is only interested in satisfying his or her own urges. A person who loves another will not want to dishonor him or her by encouraging sin.

54. Because love is patient, it will lead to what is proper. Love is always in control. In abstaining from sexual activity with a boyfriend or girlfriend, how are you honoring that person?
You are refraining from doing something that will cause the person guilt later when he or she eventually marries.

WEEK 14
SEXUAL MORALITY

DAY 1

 FOCUS

Our commitment of love, honor, and devotion toward another must be a result of Christ in us and not based on any attribute of the individual's. If we view a boyfriend or girlfriend first as a brother or sister in Christ, the relationship will be based on honor and respect. In this way, we are able to give the world a picture of what Jesus is like through our dating lives. Our thoughts must be pure if our actions in relationships are to be pure as well.

 APPLICATION

2. If your devotion to someone is based on him or her, what will be true of your devotion?
It will be limited because all human beings will inevitably fail. If, however, your devotion to another person is based on Christ, your commitment will be unconditional, just as His commitment to us is unconditional.

3. Which of the following would be ways to honor another person?
a. Consider her feelings, needs, and concerns above your own.
b. Speak positively about him to others.
c. Value her opinions and experiences.
d. Think positive, pure, and uplifting thoughts about the person.
e. Affirm the person.
f. Respect him in spite of his failures.
(Answers: all are ways of honoring another person.)

Why should we honor all people by being in awe over the mere fact of their creation?
Only people will be passing on into eternity. We should value the worth of all individuals based on this fact alone. We should realize the magnitude of the value God places on all individuals.

When was the last time you were in awe of your brother or sister? Your parents? A teacher?

4. How would it impact your relationship if you regarded your boyfriend or girlfriend as your brother or sister in Christ first, and then as your love interest?
Possible answers: I would respect her and view our relationship from the proper perspective. I would consider his interests and not merely my own regarding how the relationship would impact the person's other dating experiences, future, marriage, and so on. After you broke up, instead of hard feelings or a strained relationship, you would still care about him or her and honor or respect him/her just as you would a brother or sister.

Think through the following...
What impact does it have on a person when you break up with him or her and immediately begin dating someone else?
Possible answers: It demeans and devalues the person. It says that the relationship had little or no meaning. It takes away any element of trust that was established during the relationship.

One way to honor your future spouse is to conservatively save your kisses for him or her. Yet you may, at times, feel disappointed if you do not have and possibly have never had a boyfriend or girlfriend. How might this fact actually be the power of God working in your life, even without your realizing it?
God may actually be preventing you from participating in any kind of sexual activity in order to protect you and therefore enable you to honor your future spouse in this way.

When you know someone has participated in sexual activity, is it OK to discuss this with others? Isn't a bad reputation just one consequence of sin?
It is never acceptable or right to condemn another person in his or her sin or to gossip about it. We are

not in a position to do so since we are as guilty of sin as anyone else. When your sibling is guilty of wrong-doing, you want to protect him or her from the condemnation of others. It should be the same with your brother or sister in Christ.

Imagine the opportunity...
What are common problems that exist in the relationships of couples in high school who are dating?
Possible answers: arguing, petty jealousy, sexual activity

DAY 2

 **FOCUS**

Many in our society view marriage as void of commitment, yet God considers the union of a husband and wife so sacred that the Bible compares it to the union of Christ and the church. Just as God is unconditionally committed to us, He expects us to be unconditionally committed to our marriage partner. Sexual experiences before marriage carry with them guilt and defile the future marriage bed in many ways. We must first be a person of honor if we are to find a future spouse who is a person of honor.

 APPLICATION

8. God sees the potential of all marital relationships. What does the Bible compare marriage to?
The faithfulness and commitment God demonstrates in His relationship with us. When we are His children, nothing we can do will destroy His commitment to us. God does not demand anything of us in our marital relationships that He is not willing to demonstrate in His relationship with us.

In a spiritual sense, why do you think God hates divorce, as He declares in Malachi 2:16?
God intended for the union of a husband and wife to be like the union of Christ and His bride, the church.

12. Do you want your future spouse, who is now formulating guidelines for dating, to...
• spend time thinking about sexual sin?
• have a casual view of relationships, demonstrated through a string of girlfriends or boyfriends?
• casually throw around the words "I love you" to whomever he or she dates?
• choose relationships from impure motives, such as dating someone just to make another person jealous?

13. How can we recognize a person of honor?
We can recognize him or her only if we are a person of honor.

ELLIOT QUOTATION
Being discriminating and selective in your choice of dates has a price. Is it worth it to be dateless on Friday and Saturday nights? Is it worth it to never have even experienced a kiss from a boyfriend or girlfriend? Is it worth it to go without a prom date? Is your relationship and your commitment to your future spouse worth the sacrifice?

What would most people have to admit they initially look for in someone they are interested in dating?
The person's appearance

When you are in the midst of a long-term (probably married) relationship with a person, what are you likely to end up seeing whenever you look at him or her? Will it be his or her looks that get your attention?
You will end up seeing and valuing what a person is like on the inside. Regardless of his or her appearance, you will focus on his/her character and put little emphasis on that person's looks.

How might "group dating" be advantageous?
Group dating gives you the opportunity to learn what a person is like, how he or she responds to other people, his/her value systems, and so forth. You can get a better view of the whole picture at a distance rather than close up. It also prevents the pressure and temptation that would exist if you and your date were alone together.

What questions should you ask yourself regarding a person in whom you are interested, and what should you seek to learn about him or her?
Possible answers: Is he a Christian? Does she honor her parents? Does he respect his teachers? Does she have a genuine love for God? What is his attitude about church? Does she have a hunger for God?

DAY 3

 FOCUS

Fornication is sex with anyone other than the person we are married to, including premarital sex; and according to God's Word, it is sin. Although society excuses homosexuality as being genetic, it too is sin; and because we are all born with a sin nature, it is a matter of the will. As Christians, we are set free from all sin, including sexual sin. Regardless of our past failures, because of His grace, we must strive to be holy in regard to our sex lives.

APPLICATION
MOWDAY QUOTATION

When we are tempted to commit sexual sin, we are likely to look at the prospect in terms of our own sin, and probably don't think much about contributing to and encouraging sin in the other person. How can humility in a relationship prevent this?

Putting the other person's well-being above our own and having a genuine concern for the spiritual welfare of that person will result in us being less likely to participate in sexual activities, not because we do not want to sin, but because we do not want to contribute to sin in another person's life.

21. When you consider God's purpose in marriage, why is it easy to see that homosexuality is sin?

It is not the kind of sexual relationship that God intended, and anything that strays from God's intention is sin.

What should a person who truly believes he or she is homosexual do? Should the person live a lie?

The person should live according to the truth: that homosexuality is wrong. Just because a person feels inclined toward homosexuality does not mean he or she should act on it. Human beings can choose to resist temptation.

LIFE SITUATION

23. Jessica was devastated. Gerard dumped her, just like that. No warning, no explanation, and seemingly no regrets. She was ready to build her whole life around him, and now he was gone. The emptiness, loneliness, and sense of loss were overwhelming. He had told her he loved her. Maybe it was just a lie so he could get what he wanted out of her. And after a great deal of conflict followed by a great deal of guilt, she had given in. "I'll marry him some day anyway," she had thought. She had even justified it that way in her prayers. She felt God had chosen him for her. Well, that was all but out of the question now. She had heard that he had already asked Makaya out. Already!

She had lost her virginity. Her life would never be the same. Now she would have to live with the guilt for the rest of her life. And she felt her relationship with God would never be the same again.

Is Jessica's relationship with the Lord destroyed? What must she do in order to restore that relationship?

All she must do is repent. She must agree with God that what she did was wrong. She can't possibly go back and undo past wrongs; but as she confesses her sin, God will forgive her. God did not ever intend for us to live a life of guilt over any sin. His purpose is for us to be made clean in Him and reconciled to Him.

Why can Jessica approach her life and future relationships just as she would if she had never committed sexual sin with Gerard?

Once she has repented, she has been made pure. Psalm 103:12 assures us, "As far as the east is from the west, so far has He removed our transgressions from us." In Isaiah 1:18 we read, "'Come now, and let us reason together,' says the Lord, 'Though your sins are as scarlet, they will be as white as snow; though they are red like crimson, they will be like wool.'"

How might Jessica benefit from seeing Gerard's actions not as something that has made her life miserable but as a means by which God was working in her life instead?

The breakup put an end to Jessica's sexual sin and therefore the strain in her relationship with God. The Lord may have gotten Gerard out of Jessica's life for this reason. He alone knows who He has chosen to be Jessica's mate in life.

How should Jessica view her future relationships in terms of sexual considerations?

She must not fall back into the pattern she established with Gerard thinking, "I've lost my virginity anyway, so I might as well." Instead, she must view herself as pure because she has been forgiven. She must use her experiences as a reason not to fall into sexual sin instead of as an excuse to sin. She can approach future relationships as if she had never lost her virginity in the first place.

DAY 4

FOCUS

God created us for a relationship with Him and to glorify Him. Sexual immorality degrades not only our own bodies but also Christ. In joining ourselves to the

Lord, we are one with Him. Our desire for intimacy with another person teaches us that the real longing of our hearts is for the Lord.

APPLICATION

32. Some people insist that their sexual urges cannot be controlled. How does 1 John 4:4, which says, "You are from God, little children, and have overcome them; because greater is He who is in you than he who is in the world," refute this?

Satan tells us that such urges cannot be controlled, but God is greater than Satan. He would not tell us to abstain from sex outside of marriage without also giving us the ability to do so.

33. How does the Bible describe our relationship with Christ using the analogy of the marriage relationship?

Jesus is the bridegroom, and His church is the bride. (John 3:29; Rev. 21:2).

34. What is the only way sexual intimacy can fulfill a person?

When a person is one not only with his or her spouse but also with the Lord.

DAY 5

FOCUS

Because God is trustworthy and has a definite plan for each of our lives, we can trust Him with our dating lives. We must establish limits before dating, choose only Christians who share our moral values to date, and surround ourselves with other believers who share the same standards. We should seek to obey the Lord in terms of our dating relationships because, through His Son, we are already pleasing to Him.

APPLICATION

40. Some people may give in and compromise their moral values in dating situations because they feel pressured to do so. They may believe they have to compromise in order to hold on to the relationship. In such situations, who or what are they trusting with their dating lives?

They are trusting themselves and their sexuality to keep the relationship going. They are not trusting God to work His purpose in their lives.

41. When you trust in yourself to avoid temptation, relying on the fact that you are strong and can resist it, to whose voice are you listening?

You are listening to Satan, who wants you to believe you're strong when he knows how weak the flesh truly is. It is God's voice that tells you that you are weak and therefore need to be prepared.

Why do you think your best friend should be a fellow Christian?

You need the support of someone who is like-minded. You will not likely get the kind of support, godly perspective, and encouragement needed to withstand sexual temptation from a non-Christian.

Although communicating your limits to your date might seem awkward, what valuable information are you likely to learn about him or her once you do?

You will learn what his or her values are in that area, his or her commitment to God's commands, and how much he or she really values you.

What if you communicate your limits and your date decides he or she would rather not pursue a relationship with you? Would being honest so early-on have been a mistake?

No. You should be grateful to know what the person's intentions were before giving yourself a chance to become emotionally involved. Proverbs 4:23 warns us: "watch over your heart with all diligence."

42. How do you think your dating life would benefit if you made God an integral part of it through, for example, praying with your date?

Possible answers: Including God in the date makes you more aware of His presence and therefore more conscious of His commands.

ACTIVITY

Ask students to brainstorm words or phrases that come to mind when they think of the word discipline. Write answers on chart paper and call time after one minute.

Possible answers: being grounded, losing privileges, justice, anger, resentment

Next, ask students to brainstorm words or phrases that come to mind when they think of the Lord's discipline directed at them and at others.

Possible answers: just, necessary, hard to predict, hard to understand, not equally severe

Ask students to name words that come to mind when they think about self-discipline.

Possible answers: a drag, hard to follow through with, necessary if you're going to reach your goal, important

What determines your attitude regarding discipline?

Possible answers: whether the discipline is directed at me or at someone else, whether or not I see it as fair, the severity of it

If you asked a young child why his mom disciplined him, he would likely say: "So I won't do it again." While this is true when children are first learning right from wrong, what do you think is the long-term purpose of discipline?

The purpose of discipline, whether initiated by a human being or by God, is to bring the person back in line with what is right. The ultimate goal is for the person to avoid wrongdoing because of a changed heart, rather than a fear of punishment.

At the conclusion of this study, ask students to again brainstorm words and phrases that come to mind in regard to discipline, the Lord's disciple, and self-discipline to see if their perceptions have changed.

DAY 1

FOCUS

Disobedience to God's commands invites the Lord's discipline in our lives. God hates our sin and will not overlook it. His punishment may not necessarily be outward but may instead manifest itself in the inward person. The only way to avoid the discipline of the Lord is through repentance. We can be thankful for the Lord's discipline because it is a demonstration of His love and concern for us.

APPLICATION

"All I want for my kids is for them to grow up to be happy," a parent once said. Is there anything wrong with this statement?

It is doubtful that a parent would be pleased if her child grew up to be a happy career bank robber or a happy, personable murderer. Instead of wishing exclusively for happiness, a parent should also desire for her child to be a godly person who contributes productively to the world around him or her.

5. What is the significance of the fact that God visits our transgression with the rod and our iniquity with stripes?

God's anger is not directed at us, the sinners, but rather at the sin. He hates the sin, not the sinner.

CONNER QUOTATION

LIFE SITUATION

"What is it about her, anyway?" asked Colleen. "I mean, she cheats on every test she takes, and she never gets caught!"

"Allison has to cheat on her tests," said Alonzo. "She doesn't know how to do the math because Tad always does her homework for her." The others laughed ruefully.

"Well, I have to say it just makes me sick when she goes up on the stage to get her honor roll certificates every single semester." Holly couldn't hide the anger in her voice. "I mean, I study, you know, all the time; and I never get any credit for it, not even from my mom! I bet she wishes she had a daughter more like Allison."

"Well, it'll catch up to her some day, no doubt," said Tito, the voice of reason. "I mean, you can't just cheat all the time and never get caught!" He responded to the doubtful looks of his friends. "How stupid do you think Ms. Turner is anyway?"

"Pretty stupid up to this point," said Colleen.

What questions do you think go through Colleen and Holly's minds when they compare their own efforts and rewards to the efforts and rewards of Allison?
They probably question why Allison, who does wrong, continues to prosper while they, who do what is right, continue to struggle. They likely question the justice in it.

What do you think the participants in this conversation would like to see happen to Allison?
They would like to see her get caught and punished for her wrongdoing. Specifically, they would probably like to see her lose her honor roll awards and get suspended from school.

Why do you think they would like to see Allison outwardly punished?
Possible answers: Usually we want to see those who do wrong punished so it will make us feel better. We then feel like they are getting what they deserve.

When we see no outward discipline, is it safe to assume that the person guilty of willful sin is getting away with it?
No. We don't know what is going on within the person.

6. Give an example of how those in the following situations could be disciplined.
Loraine is guilty of gossiping about others.
Possible answer: She might end up being hurt by the gossip of others.
Damien has been experimenting with drugs.
Possible answer: He could get caught with the drugs and end up with a police record.
Shalisa has been taking small amounts of money out of the cash register at work.

Possible answer: She could get fired.
Danae has been lying to her friends Meg and Renee about Felicia so they will refuse to be friends with her anymore. The reason for her lies is that Danae is secretly jealous of Felicia's good looks.
Possible answer: Meg and Renee could turn on Danae instead.

DAY 2

FOCUS
The Lord disciplines those He loves: those who are His children. Therefore, we should be thankful for it. The discipline of the Lord produces righteousness in us. His purpose in it is to make us Christlike.

APPLICATION
13. Most child psychologists agree that children who are not disciplined by their parents really crave discipline, which often results in increased bad behavior in order to get attention. Why do you think this is so?
Possible answers: Limits and boundaries are set as an affirmation of the parent's love, care, and concern. In other words, we associate love and concern with boundaries and discipline.

15. If God did not discipline us, how would this reflect on the role He would play in our lives?
He would be distant. He would have little concern for our welfare. He would not be demonstrating His love for us.

18. How could we respond to the Lord's discipline?
We could respond with questioning, bitterness, resentment, rebellion.

20. Do you think it would be possible to become Christlike without being disciplined by the Lord? Why or why not?
No. Because if we never experienced negative consequences as a result of our sin, we might tend to choose the sin over godliness.

DAY 3

FOCUS
God's plan for His people is for good. We must learn to put our trust in the Lord and not in the blessings He provides us. Disobedience leads to His discipline while seeking Him in obedience prevents the need

for it. Our greatest need—a relationship with Him—was provided through His Son. We must remain disciplined in seeking God whether we are experiencing a modern-day wilderness in our lives or a modern-day promised land.

APPLICATION

25. "I feel closer to God when things are going well for me than I do when things are going bad because I'm so happy and thankful during the good times." What is wrong with this statement? How does it relate to you?

This person is putting her trust in the Lord's blessings, the good things in life, rather than in God Himself, who is working in her life regardless of the circumstances. She needs to learn to be thankful for the discipline and trials, which lead to godliness, and to trust God in His wisdom. We, too, must look at discipline as something that is good because it brings us back in line with God's original plan for our lives.

DAY 4

FOCUS

Self-discipline is planned, regular, and proactive. We train ourselves to be godly through disciplining ourselves to pursue godliness. We must also use self-discipline as a shield against any form of temptation. Discipline in pursuing Christlikeness is not just beneficial for the moment or for the duration of our lives; it is also profitable for all eternity.

APPLICATION

36. What contradiction do you hear in the following statements?

"Spend your time in the exercise of watching your favorite movie."

"Discipline yourself to participate in your favorite hobby."

"Take the time to indulge yourself in eating your favorite foods."

"Train yourself to buy whatever you want for yourself."

Little or no self-discipline is required to do the things we enjoy—the things we would do if there were no rules about what we should or could do. Self-discipline is what we exert when our very nature or desires would dictate that we do otherwise.

Which words do you associate with self-discipline?
a. Deliberate
b. Depends on your mood
c. Consistent
d. Passive
e. Debatable
f. Active
g. Scheduled
h. A commitment
i. Depends on your energy
(Answers: a, c, f, g, h)

38. A soldier must train himself to fight in battle. A pilot must be trained to fly an airplane, and a surgeon must be trained in the latest surgical techniques. How must Christians train themselves to be godly? What specific tools must they use?

Possible answers: through reading, studying, and memorizing God's Word; through daily prayer and quiet time; through fellowshipping with other believers. The key is to practice each of these things on a regular basis and not merely in a haphazard, "when-I'm-in-the-mood," or "when-I-have-the-time" manner.

40. Persons malnourished in the physical sense don't eat nutritious food, or any food at all, on a regular basis. How can we be malnourished in our spiritual lives?

By not having a steady, daily intake of spiritual things

How might we limit our spiritual nourishment to merely junk food?

Possible answers: participating in church-related activities for fun with no desire to learn and grow; spending a worship service thinking about school, friends, conversations; limiting our reading of spiritual material solely to Christian fiction.

41. How is discipline confused with godliness?

Some people believe their self-control results in godliness. For example, they may believe that not eating certain foods on certain days of the week will make them godly. In reality, God is the One who creates godliness through our discipline of applying Scripture to daily living.

44. Look again at the rewards you rated as either a 4 or a 5. If, for example, you rated money or a salary highly, how must you discipline yourself in order to obtain it?

You have to get out of bed when the alarm goes off. You must get to work on time. You must give up leisurely activities you could participate in if you were not working.

How does this relate to your self-discipline when it comes to spending time with God?
You have to do the same things. If you are disciplined, you will seek Him whether you are tired or not, when you want to go to the mall instead, and so forth.

When is it easiest to exercise self-discipline? When is it the most difficult?
Most people would say that self-discipline is easy when the reward is desirable; in other words, when we are externally (and in some cases internally) motivated. Self-discipline is difficult when the task at hand is not appealing or we are not motivated to accomplish it.

46. If you choose to sleep late instead of going to Sunday School, for example, how would you benefit from your choice physically?
You would be more rested and more alert.

If you choose to get up and go to Sunday School, how would you benefit from your choice?
You would receive long-term benefits in the form of being ministered to, being encouraged, and growing spiritually, which impacts the realm of eternity.

How does our self-discipline in this area relate to Jesus' command in Luke 9:23: "If anyone wishes to come after Me, let him deny himself, and take up his cross daily, and follow Me"?
He tells us to deny ourselves, which means to give up those fleshly things (like additional sleep) that will hinder our commitment to follow Him.

DAY 5

 FOCUS
A disciplined believer is diligent and fervent in serving the Lord. The disciplined will be rewarded, but there are no long-term rewards for the undisciplined. The accountability of others can help us to have a disciplined walk with God, but our ultimate accountability must be with Him alone.

 APPLICATION
50. What are the earthly rewards of self-discipline, hard work, and persistence?
In many cases wealth, power, recognition or fame

What are the earthly rewards for the lack of self-discipline? What is the cost?
The rewards are brief, fleeting, momentary pleasures. The cost is the loss of long-term rewards.

Proverbs 13:4
Complete the following sentences in the same manner in which a "sluggard" would complete them:
a. "I wish I could make better grades, but..."
b. "I would like to go to college, but..."
c. "I wish I could fit into a smaller size, but..."
d. "I sure would like to have a car like his, but..."
Possible answers: a–"I would have to spend too much time studying." b–"I sure don't want to spend four or five more years of my life in school!" c–"I don't want to stop eating sweets or have to exercise." d–"I would have to find an after-school job."

ELLIOT QUOTATION
What inference can you draw from the fact that the word disciple and the word discipline are so similar?
The disciple is to learn through discipline. You cannot expect to be a disciple of Christ and leave your learning up to chance or mere life experience.

52. Messing up a room is easy. Cleaning it up is much more difficult. Watching TV and talking on the telephone are easy. Becoming Christlike is more difficult. Why is this?
Becoming Christlike, like cleaning up a room, requires work.

What happens to a garden that is never weeded?
It will not produce pretty flowers or delicious vegetables. Instead, they will whither and die.

56. Which of the following are other persons certain to do?
a. disappoint   b. sin   c. fail   d. change   e. die
All of the above. Only God will never disappoint, never sin, never fail, never change, and never die.

 ACTIVITY
Ask students to brainstorm words or phrases that come to mind when they think of the word discipline. Write answers on chart paper and call time after one minute.

Next, ask students to brainstorm words or phrases that come to mind when they think of the Lord's discipline directed at them and at others.

Ask students to name words that come to mind when they think about self-discipline.

WEEK 16
TAMING THE TONGUE

INSTRUCTIONS TO THE LEADER:

On Day 2, you will find an activity in which students are encouraged to role-play situations where the tongue is used for evil purposes. One example is given and could be demonstrated, impromptu, by two students. They could, however, create the dialogue themselves for other situations based on the Scripture reference given. If you choose to have students role-play in this manner, it would be beneficial to prepare for this in advance of the Discipleship class, with the students ready to present their scenarios at the designated point in the discussion.

DAY 1

FOCUS

Although the tongue is a small part of the body, its power is great. From our mouths come both blessing and cursing, yet as bitter water pollutes the fresh water, so the bad corrupts the good.

APPLICATION

Proverbs 18:21 "Death and life are in the power of the tongue. . ." It might be tempting to think that this applies only to kings or dictators who have the power to put someone to death at any inclination, or the words of a governor who grants clemency at the last moment to someone on death row. But actually, every day our tongues are capable of producing both death and life. How is this possible?

Possible answers: The tongue gives life when it heals emotional wounds, uplifts, encourages. However, the tongue is just as capable of producing emotional death when it criticizes, degrades, or insults.

SWINDOLL QUOTATION

What are examples of other tools that are a necessity to our lives but could be detrimental if used incorrectly?

Possible answers: knives, a car, gasoline for heating homes and keeping automobiles running, etc.

5. After praying for a lost friend during the invitation of a worship service, Jackie sang the concluding hymn of praise. As she stuffed her bulletin into her Bible and prepared to leave, she nudged her friend Jolynn and said, "Look at that. I didn't notice Nicole over there. I mean, what's she doing here? Trying to come across as a good girl or something? It's not like everybody doesn't know better or anything!"

What is the problem with this scenario?
Jackie is praising God in prayer and song and interceding for a lost friend with the same lips she is using to speak negatively and further rumors about another person. It is bitter water and fresh water coming out of the same opening.

6. What do you think happens when bitter water and fresh water are combined?
The fresh water will become bitter also.

How does that relate to our attempts to "talk out of both sides of our mouths"?
We will be known by our bitter water, not by the fresh. The negative things we say will make the positive things seem insincere.

7. Explain how the following "weapons of death" are like the power our tongues have to destroy others:
a. stabbing
The pain of a knife wound would be like the pain, the "sting" left when someone hurts another with his or her words. It can be quick, crippling, and permanent. Even if the wound heals, a scar still remains which reminds the person of the hurt that caused it.
b. disease
As is true of words that hurt, pain is inevitable with disease. Long after the initial contact with the germ, the symptoms still persist. Although the symptoms can be temporarily treated, the disease remains.

c. a bullet

It pierces the heart and causes a quick yet painful death. A bullet is expelled from a gun with ease yet renders devastating effects.

d. starvation

This is a slow and painful death. Consistent verbal abuse kills slowly and over time. A person who is the victim of it becomes like an empty shell, completely zapped of esteem, hope, and the will to survive.

e. car accident

It is something unexpected, yet in an instant it wounds, maims, or kills. The victim of verbal abuse is never the same again, just as the victim of a car accident may be changed through paralysis, disfigurement, or recurrent pain.

f. smoking

Both negative words and cigarette smoke are repulsive to others. It has the capability of hurting the smoker as well as spreading its ill effects to those around him or her. The longer smoking persists, like verbal abuse, the greater the potential is for long-term ill effects.

8. How are sins of the tongue a "cancer"?

They may begin as a small incident or casual or careless remark, but they feed on themselves and continue to grow. Soon, the disease spreads throughout a person's entire being. The more it becomes a part of him or her, the more difficult it is to cure.

SPURGEON QUOTATION

When someone is speaking negatively about a fellow Christian, what would be a better alternative to "jumping on the bandwagon"?

A better alternative would be to remain silent or to attempt to counter an attack with a positive word.

DAY 2

 **FOCUS**

Boasting in evil, devising destruction, and false words are examples of bitter water when it comes to our speech. Although the words of humans are evil, the Lord's Words are true and perfect. We should never allow unwholesome words to proceed from our mouths, but only words that encourage and benefit.

APPLICATION

9. Words are not the only thing that can be compared to fresh water or bitter water. The attitude and tone with which they are stated can be fresh or bitter as well. For example, how could the following statement be said in a manner consistent with fresh water, and how could it be stated as bitter water? "He's the smartest guy in the class."

When stated sincerely, this comment comes forth as fresh water. When said in a sarcastic manner, for example, this statement becomes bitter.

 ACTIVITY

Select one of the indications of bitter water described in Psalm 52:1-4 and create a one or two-minute scenario in which it is portrayed.

Example: Psalm 52:2: the tongue devises destruction

Earl: Drake thinks he's so cool. I'm sick of being benched so he can be a first-stringer just because his dad's a coach.

Kent: No joke, man . . . Let's do something about it.

Earl: Like what ya got in mind?

Kent: Oh, I don't know . . . maybe, uh, do a little damage to that new car of his. . .

Earl: (smiling) . . . Oh yeah, he is so proud of that thing. Well let's just show him a thing or two about fair play. How about a good old tire slashing?

(The two guys walk off laughing)

14. How can positive words be evil?

They are evil when they are insincere or improperly or impurely motivated.

16. Indicate which of the following examples of bitter water in speaking you recognize as those common among you and your peer group:

a. speaking falsehood   b. boasting

c. devising destruction   d. deceit

e. criticism   f. filthy language

g. dirty jokes   h. harsh words

What fresh water would be better alternatives?

Possible answers: sincere words, encouragement, praise, speaking the truth, gentle words of kindness.

DAY 3

 FOCUS

Although some circumstances or people cause us to think before we speak, it is the careless words we utter without thought that demonstrate the true condition of our hearts. A person's heart will determine his or her thoughts, words, and finally actions.

APPLICATION

19. Anyone can make his or her speech sound good for the particular moment or for a certain person. If you were going on a job interview or being counseled by your pastor, for example, how would your speech be different than it would be if you were just hanging out with your friends?

You would be more likely to think before you spoke and tailor your words to sound impressive or sincere.

21. If we were to record our words for a given period of time, we might be surprised at how many careless words roll off our tongues without even a thought. Upon playing back the tape, what might our words tell us about ourselves?

They might give us an idea of what evil exists on the inside: anger, bitterness, jealousies. Our words also reveal the condition of our relationship with God.

If a person claims to love you, how might his or her speech contradict the words, "I love you"?

Although a person may say, "I love you," if he or she gossips about you behind your back, lies to you, or attempts to deceive you with words, his or her words of love have little value (Ephesians 4:25).

23. What is the best way to reach the point where you don't necessarily have to "think" before you speak in order to bring forth what is good?

The more you fill yourself with God, the less you will have to think before you speak.

DAY 4

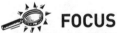

FOCUS

As Christians, often the sins to which we are most vulnerable are those of the tongue, including gossip. We may even tend to spiritualize gossip under the label of prayer requests and Christian concern. Like David who suffered greatly because of those who spoke against him, we must return good for evil when others speak negatively about us. This is the response of Christ.

APPLICATION

27. According to Psalm 50:19-20 and Proverbs 11:9, if a person's heart is not right, is there anyone for whom he or she will draw the line when it comes to gossip?

No. Not even his or her own brother or neighbor.

28. As Christians, we are most vulnerable to sins of the tongue. How is this fact actually an indication of our placing our efforts and emphasis on the self?

When we gossip about others, it puts us in the center of attention because others are always eager to listen. It makes people feel important when they know something about someone else and in a subtle way it makes them feel better about themselves when they have something negative to say about someone else.

Nonbelievers may look at Christians who are backbiting, criticizing, and degrading other Christians with their words and draw conclusions about Christianity based on what they hear. After all, Christians are supposed to be different, right? But what does the Bible say about the religion of those who do not bridle their tongues?

Their religion is worthless. It does not give others an accurate picture of what Christ is like.

How can we train our tongues in the other direction?

As Christians, we need to focus on the good things happening to others. Instead of seeking to know and repeat what is bad, we should focus on telling others about the awards, achievements, opportunities, and positive characteristics of a person. In this way, our words will be encouraging and uplifting rather than destructive and hurtful.

29. How might a person who gossips be tempted to minimize his or her words to the one he or she spoke about? Of what is this an indication?

He or she might say, "I was only teasing," or "she just misunderstood what I said," or this person might deny saying anything in the first place. This is an indication of an impure heart.

32. A person could justify listening to gossip by stating that he or she wouldn't tell anyone else. After all, who is hurt by your knowing if you don't repeat it? Yet what would actually be the better alternative?

It would be better not to listen to the gossip in the first place. Knowing gossip about someone else affects a person negatively, creating in him or her a negative attitude toward the person, for example.

35. Sometimes we can be very naive when it comes to gossip. We hang around with a circle of friends in which, Nelson is gossiping about Sal and Ashley, and Rick is saying negative things about his best friend Willis. We may participate in it willingly and thrive on knowing the dirty little details of everyone's life, yet what simple fact might we be overlooking?

Your circle of friends who are all gossiping about each other are gossiping about you too.

What will inevitably happen in this situation?
Your eyes will be opened to the pain that gossip can cause when you're on the receiving end of its sting.

DAY 5

FOCUS

If we guard our tongues, we can avoid sin and the inevitable consequences of it. Those who not only discipline their tongues, but also speak what is godly, give life to those around them. When used correctly and in the right circumstances, our words have the ability to minister to others.

APPLICATION

LIFE SITUATION

43. Dominique knew that Blair had been smoking marijuana with Rusty, her boyfriend, for a couple of months now. She also knew that, in spite of his faults, Adrienne had wanted to go out with Rusty for as long as she could remember. Dominique felt sorry for Adrienne. All she needed was a chance to start dating a cool guy like Rusty. She would be a good influence on him. She wouldn't give in to his bad habits the way Blair did.

Adrienne had a good relationship with Blair's parents. Their families had been friends for years, even though Blair and Adrienne never quite hit it off the way everyone else seemed to. From what Dominique knew of Blair's family, her parents were very conservative and very strict when it came to Blair's boyfriends. If they only knew what Rusty was really like. . .

What might Dominique be tempted to do in this situation?
She might decide to tell Adrienne that Blair had been smoking marijuana with Rusty, and then suggest to Adrienne that she mention it to Blair's parents.

What might she hope to achieve by spreading the information?
She might hope that Blair's parents would force her to break up with Rusty, and then Adrienne could have a chance to date him.

How, instead, might Dominique determine to "muzzle" her mouth and put devious lips far from her?
She should not discuss with Adrienne, or anyone else, what Blair and Rusty have been doing. She should keep her lips from spreading gossip.

Assume Dominique decided to tell Adrienne that Blair had been smoking marijuana with Rusty, and that Adrienne, in turn, revealed the information to Blair's parents. What would be the result if she later discovered that the person who told her about Blair and Rusty had misunderstood his own source, and Blair and Rusty had never smoked marijuana at all; it had been another couple all together?
Then Dominique would have seriously hurt two innocent people because of her gossip and her unwillingness to abandon the quarrel before it broke out. Friendships would inevitably be damaged or lost.

44. Proverbs 12:14: When a man yields "fruit" from the words of his mouth, what is he giving to those around him?
He gives life, instead of death, to those around him. It takes life to produce fruit.

Proverbs 21:23: When a person uses his or her mouth to get into trouble, for what must he or she then use his or her mouth? What's often the result?
Then the person must use his or her mouth in order to try to get out of trouble. Unfortunately, the situation often just gets worse. It would have been better if he or she had guarded his or her mouth and tongue in the first place.

48. When might words spoken in right circumstances need to be courageous?
When the person to whom the words are directed is not likely to be receptive to them.

How might a person's attitude be affected if our words are filled with genuine concern?
The person is more likely to be receptive to what we have to say if he or she feels that we care about him or her and are genuinely concerned.

Can words spoken in right circumstances be kind and encouraging, but lack sincerity? Can they be courageous and timely but lack kindness? What is the key to words that bring forth fruit?
All significant elements must exist in order for the words to bring forth fruit.

52. How many of your conversations produce fruit?

WEEK 17
CHRISTIAN CONDUCT AND A GODLY DISPOSITION

DAY 1

 **FOCUS**

Our responsiveness to the commands of our consciences determines our behavior. Paul's conscience testified that his conduct was holy and sincere. As Christians, we seek to obey God's laws, and not just acceptable standards of morality. When our conscience warns us of wrongdoing, we must heed it as the Holy Spirit's conviction.

 **APPLICATION**

2 Corinthians 1:12
Why is it important to remember that our holiness and godly sincerity are not a result of our own wisdom, but are only a result of God's grace?
Non-Christians can conduct themselves in sincerity, kindness, and morality. Godliness and holiness can only truly be achieved through knowing Christ. And it is only through God's grace that we are able to know Him in the first place.

2. What are the shortcomings that result when we behave in a certain way not because it is right, but because we don't want to feel guilty if we don't?
In such a situation, our motives for doing the right thing are weak. There is very little likelihood that this attitude will sustain us through all temptation.

WHITE QUOTATION
If we refuse to listen to the voice of our conscience when it tells us we have done something wrong, we are likely to find it easier to ignore it the next time. Can you think of an example of this "watered down" guilt?
Possible answers: When you are a small child and you hear someone utter a bad word, you are likely to be shocked and even appalled. Yet as you are exposed to more bad words, and maybe even start to use a few of them yourself, you become less bothered by them. Another example is sexual immorality. As you give in to the temptation to go a little farther, your feelings and emotions tell you that what you are experiencing is better than what your conscience is telling you. The more your sexual sin progresses, the less guilt you feel over earlier compromises.

ALDRICH QUOTATION
How must we also resist the urge to try and become someone else's conscience?
If another believer's conscience permits him or her to participate in something while ours does not, we must not accuse or condemn him or her for it.

DAY 2

 FOCUS

Although the world sees a person with wealth, talent, or beauty as one who is blessed, the value system Jesus taught in His Sermon on the Mount sharply contrasts this view. Friendship with the world is hostility toward God. Those who are less advantaged on earth are greatly advantaged in God's kingdom when they choose to rely on Him to meet their needs.

 **APPLICATION**

9E. How is showing mercy to another person self-rewarding?
Showing mercy and forgiving another, even when he or she does not ask for it or deserve it, is freeing. Holding a grudge and harboring bitterness turns the anger inward. It never allows for peace.

DAY 3

FOCUS

A person who uses his or her tongue for grumbling or arguing reveals an ungodly disposition. The Bible instructs us to rejoice, give thanks in all things, and pray without ceasing. In so doing, we will take on a godly disposition and become children of God who are lights in the world.

APPLICATION

12. Which of the following are characteristics of a "grumbler"?

a. complaining
b. belittling the efforts of others
c. gossiping
d. never satisfied
e. looks for the bad in things
f. never takes the blame
g. discontented
h. never pleased
i. negative

(All are characteristics of a grumbler.)

LIFE SITUATION

It was Monday morning, and Marcos had stayed up very late the night before studying for his history test. His teacher, Mr. Dawson, was notorious for assigning several chapters worth of material to go over, study in depth, and memorize, and then asking very specific, seemingly unimportant questions on the test. It was almost as if he wanted to trip you up. Marcos couldn't help but feel frustrated and defeated before he took the test. Everyone else in the class felt the same way too.

"It makes me mad just thinking about how stupid this test is gonna be," complained Pam. "I've spent the last three nights studying for this and I know it's not gonna do me one bit of good."

"I wouldn't even waste my time," said Desmond. "I mean, what good does it do to study when you're just gonna make an F anyway, right?"

"Maybe if enough people complain we can get Dawson fired!" said Carter. "Yeah, that's my major goal in life: to see him axed!"

"You know what really bugs me?" Kent asked. "At least if he asked, you know, the big stuff I could use a cheat sheet. But there's no way to cheat on the kind of questions he asks!"

Marcos felt just as frustrated as the others. How could he deny his emotions and instead give them a picture of what Jesus is like?

Marcos could remove himself from the conversation and say nothing. He could quietly work on his test and refuse to talk bad about Mr. Dawson regardless of the outcome. He could even say something positive to the others regarding their teacher, or make a remark that would make their efforts seem more positive, such as the fact that because Mr. Dawson expects them to know the information in such great detail, they are forced to put more effort into their studies which means they will gain more knowledge in the end. He must follow the instructions of Philippians 2:14 and "Do all things without grumbling or disputing."

13. Which of the following are characteristics of an "arguer"?

a. picks fights
b. must have the last word
c. keeps things "stirred up"
d. disagreeable
e. challenges the opinions of others
f. defensive
g. negative
h. often unapproachable
i. places importance on trivial things

(All are characteristics of an arguer.)

LIFE SITUATION

15. Carl hadn't exactly had a good day. . . or a good week, for that matter. He couldn't seem to get along with his wife. She just didn't understand him. She didn't even try to. Every time he turned around, someone was making him mad: the neighbor who insisted on using the noisy leaf blower too early in the morning; his friend Dale who borrowed things but never seemed to return them; his kids who just couldn't seem to get along with each other. It seemed like he had a problem with nearly everyone he knew. And that stupid pharmacist! All he needed was a simple prescription filled and he ended up having to wait over an hour for it just because the lady put the form in the wrong tray!

"I can't believe you could be so dumb!" he had yelled at the woman. "Don't you think I have things to do too? It's not like I have an extra hour to wait around for you to figure out how to do your job or anything! My four-year-old wouldn't make that kind of mistake!"

Now he would have to skip dinner in order to go visiting a church prospect with his fellow deacon, Ronald

Simpson. He didn't want to do it anyway, but it was something deacons were expected to do. He raced into the church just in time to receive his prospect card. It said, "Jenilee Peterson" on 18th and Vandever. "Jenilee Peterson," Carl thought. "That name sure sounds familiar. . ." He felt his face flush as he realized that this was the name he had read on the pharmacist's I. D. tag barely an hour earlier.

Carl went ahead and visited the pharmacist with his friend Ronald. The pharmacist was friendly and courteous, but she obviously recognized Carl from their earlier confrontation. It was good for Carl to invite her to come to church, but how do you think he might actually have torn down more than what he had built up?
The pharmacist would not be likely to be receptive to Carl's invitation to attend church after the way she had been treated. In fact, Jenilee Peterson could have been turned off to church and Christianity all together.

Why do you think Carl didn't just overlook the pharmacist's mistake and bite his tongue when he was tempted to yell at her?
Carl's difficulty getting along with others is evidence of his argumentative spirit. He didn't overlook the mistake because he chose not to.

How will Carl's argumentative spirit ultimately affect him?
He will alienate others if he does not change. A person who chooses not to think before he or she speaks and therefore has no control over emotions such as anger will have difficulty in relationships because once words are spoken, they can't be taken back. The damage is done and it is the argumentative person who is left to deal with the consequences.

16. If Carl, in the above life situation, had chosen to overlook the inconvenience the pharmacist's mistake had caused him and instead found a reason to be thankful for the delay, what would have been the result?
He could have been a positive witness instead of a negative one. The woman would have remembered his patience and understanding, which are characteristics of Christ. She may have been drawn to Christ as a result.

17. What characteristics will describe a person who is a light in his or her world?
Possible answers: joyful, kind, energetic, optimistic,

refreshing. These are characteristics that are within and cannot be hidden on the outside.

The stars that shine brightly in the sky are examples of lights in our world. How can our light be compared to theirs?
Possible answers: Stars are used for navigational purposes. When we do all things without grumbling and disputing, and therefore reflect the light of Christ, others may look to us, and ultimately to Him, for guidance and direction in their own lives. Together, stars form constellations which are pictures that represent particular objects, such as the big and little dippers, and together Christians give others a picture of Christ when they reflect His light in their conduct and disposition. Stars reflect light in the midst of an otherwise dark world.

18. If we were to be honest, we would probably all have to admit to being guilty of grumbling or arguing over all of the areas in this list and more. Why do you think this is so?
Possible answers: Grumbling is a result of self-centeredness. We complain when we are inconvenienced or our pride is threatened or injured. It can be a manifestation of laziness, intolerance, or a lack of concern or consideration for others. It can also be habit-forming.

DAY 4

 FOCUS
When we are saved, God creates in us an attitude of repentance of sin, hope in His calling, and a godly lifestyle when we submit to His Lordship. Paul encourages specific characteristics of godliness, including purity, dignity, and sound speech. In following the directions for Christian conduct, we honor God's Word and make the doctrine of God attractive to others.

APPLICATION
21. Paul gives instructions regarding conduct to specific groups, including older men and older women. Yet how can his instructions to them actually be advice to all of us?
Everyone should have older role models to look up to, especially spiritual ones. The truth is that we are almost always in a position in life when we are an older role model to someone. For instance, elementary school-aged children look up to and are greatly

influenced by high school students. Therefore, high school students can serve as positive role models when they are living a lifestyle consistent with Paul's instructions.

When participating in a sports event with team members who use vulgar language, what does the guy who is committed to Christian conduct do?
He remains sound in speech which is beyond reproach. He doesn't "join in."

When friends encourage a young Christian woman to go out drinking with them, how does she respond?
She avoids alcohol and the circumstances that would lead to temptation. She doesn't go along.

When a Christian guy who leads a very busy life is tempted to "blow off" his history assignments, since memorizing medieval names and dates will never benefit him later in life, what does he do?
He is sensible; he knows that failing to do assignments will hurt him (and his grade point) in the long run. And he does his work heartily as for the Lord rather than men.

When a young lady who desires to live a godly life is pressured into compromising sexually with her boyfriend, and she finds that she would really like to compromise, what does she do?
She chooses to remain sensible and pure and honor God and her future husband by refusing to give in to the temptation.

25. Godliness involves basing what we do or think on what God says. In any situation, what are examples of questions we might ask ourselves that would benefit us in our Christian conduct?
Possible answers: Is this my solution or God's solution? Is it the way I would choose to respond or the way Christ would respond? Is it what I desire or what God desires?

DAY 5

 **FOCUS**

Loving all of our brethren is the aim of the Christian life. We cannot be godly people without loving others because God is the source of love. Our ambition must be to lead a quiet, gentle life, work with our hands, and depend not on other human beings, but only on God who is the source of all that is good.

 **APPLICATION**

28. We are supposed to love all of the brethren, yet there are some people who are more difficult to love than others. How can we possibly love all people, regardless of their personal flaws?
We have to separate the person from the behavior that is difficult to accept. In other words, through Christ we can love the person without loving or even accepting ungodly behavior. Sometimes we think God is not big enough to handle the person without our help, when the truth is that we are instructed to love him or her while He is the one to convict the person of sin.

What do you think is beneficial to keep in mind about ourselves when we think we can't tolerate someone we are instructed to love?
Christ tolerates us in spite of our faults. How can we not tolerate what we don't like in others when He does?

31. The world does not advocate unconditional love. What kind of "love" does the world seem to condone?
Possible answers: Love someone only when it is reciprocated. Love someone only if he or she makes you happy. Love someone only if he or she deserves it. Love someone as long as he or she treats you right.

35. What is the benefit of working with your hands to Christian conduct?
It keeps us occupied in service. It keeps our minds focused on a project and not distracted by sin: meddling in other people's business, lusts of the flesh, etc. It allows character qualities to be enriched as we perform wholeheartedly, joyfully, patiently, etc., and with the right motives.

36. Why must we not put our dependence in other human beings, but only in God?
Other human beings will fail and disappoint, but God never fails, never disappoints, and never changes. God is the source of all things we have and ever will have. We must only depend on humans as far as they point us to God.

WEEK 18
PATIENCE, KINDNESS, GOODNESS

DAY 1

FOCUS

Patience, kindness, goodness are the fruit of the Spirit which all Christians possess. God's very nature is a reflection of this fruit. In Christ is life, and it is only life that produces fruit. The Lord desires to be gracious to us, but because He is just, He allows us to reap the consequences of our sin.

APPLICATION

2. Because of Christ, we are able to experience the kind of patience, kindness, goodness that are only possible with God. Why is this true?

The fruit of the Spirit always produces life. Patience, kindness, and goodness are only possible in Christ.

5. Why will God allow us to reap the consequences of our sin, instead of patiently tolerating it?

He is not only patient, but He is also just. Therefore, He allows us to reap the consequences of our sin in order to discipline us and bring us back to Him.

6. While God longs to be gracious to us, what do we often long for when we see the sins of others?

We long for them to get what they deserve.

DAY 2

FOCUS

Patience is needed in waiting on the Lord and His timing to work out His will in our lives. Other people must also be the object of our patience and tolerance. The real fruit of patience has been cultivated in our lives when we are patient with everyone in circumstances that caused us to lose our patience in the past. We must endure the imperfections in others, just as God endures the imperfections in us.

APPLICATION

8. Why do you think a farmer waits patiently for his crops to grow? How does this apply to our lives?

He is helpless to hurry up the process. And because he does not know which seeds will take root and grow and which ones will not, he must rely solely on God's intervention to cause the growth. We must wait patiently on the Lord because ultimately He has control over circumstances we could never control.

10. The verses in question 10 from the study explain the benefits of waiting on the Lord. What are the benefits of taking control yourself?

There are no benefits to being in control. We may think that taking control of our lives (which the world strongly advocates) is the key to success, but according to these verses, we obtain strength, God's goodness, and exaltation when we give God control of our lives and then patiently wait on His timing. And when we allow the Lord's will to become a reality in our lives, we will be blessed (Jeremiah 29:11).

11. What kind of a life will we naturally lead when we are in control?

We will naturally lead a sinful life. It is human nature to choose sin.

What are some reasons why we choose to take control ourselves?

Possible answers: lack of patience, thinking we can "speed up" the process, misconceptions about God, such as thinking He isn't interested in working out the details of our lives, etc.

Question 11 states that waiting on the Lord is an issue of faith. How likely are we to please God when we choose not to wait on Him?

It is impossible to please Him when we take control because without faith, it is impossible to please Him (Hebrews 11:6).

DAY 3

 FOCUS

Kindness is the Holy Spirit's influence within us that causes us to be sensitive to the needs of others, while goodness is the action that follows. Sharing Christ with a friend is the best way to fulfill his or her greatest need. Kindness from Christian friends in times of despair can encourage the person and help prevent him or her from forsaking God. The kindness that originates from the Holy Spirit is not only extended to those we love, but it is selflessly and submissively extended to our enemies as well.

APPLICATION

LIFE SITUATION

20. Taryn desperately wanted to be captain of the cheerleading squad. She had been a cheerleader the year before, and she felt like she would be a good leader for this year's squad. Her heart was pounding as the announcement was made regarding who would be captain. When she did not hear her name, her heart fell. But disappointment turned to shock as she continued to hear the list read of those who would be cheerleaders for the upcoming school year. As so many others around her rejoiced and celebrated their successes, the awful truth began to sink in: She didn't make captain. She didn't even make the cheerleading squad at all.

How do you think Taryn felt?
Possible answers: devastated, like a failure, embarrassed, humiliated, angry, etc.

Taryn's good friend Kate did not feel compassion for Taryn. She didn't feel sorry for her at all. Why do you think her response to Taryn's devastation could have been so uncaring?
Possible answers: Kate could have been envious of Taryn's position on the cheerleading squad the year before. Taryn could have been proud and conceited prior to tryouts, bragging that she would be captain. Taryn may have shown little compassion toward Kate in the past in similar situations, etc.

Last year when Taryn made the cheerleading squad and her friend Kate did not, Taryn started to feel like maybe Kate wasn't worthy of being a good friend after all. She started spending less time with Kate, who had been her best friend for years, and started spending more and more time with her cheerleader friends. Taryn became conceited and made Kate feel inferior when she commented on her "clumsiness" and "lack of school spirit." Knowing this, do you think Kate was justified in her response to Taryn's lack of success?
Possible answers: Most people would say that she was probably justified in lacking compassion because of Taryn's actions in the past.

**When a believer observes that. . .
What else, besides "It's not my problem" do believers sometimes use as excuses to avoid aiding another believer who is despairing?**
Possible answers: "There's not really anything I can do about it anyway." "I have too many problems of my own to spend time worrying about someone else's." Not really having compassion on the person in the first place, etc.

SANDERSON QUOTATION
Although it may be tempting to offer advice along the lines of, "If I were you, I would. . ." to a friend who is in despair, what would be a better approach and also an indication of greater spiritual health?
It would be better to encourage another with godly counsel. God's Words are always superior to our own.

27. **Think of someone in your life right now who does not deserve your kindness. Maybe it is someone who has been unkind, unfair, or even cruel to you. What are some ways you could extend the type of kindness that asks nothing in return and requires complete humility and submission?**

DAY 4

 FOCUS

Goodness is a fruit we must cultivate in our lives because we were created for good works in Christ. The goodness of the Holy Spirit is different from the goodness of the world because its selfless purpose is to glorify God, and never for any personal gain or glory. In doing good to other believers, we encourage and support them in their walk with Christ. Every small act of goodness we perform will be rewarded.

APPLICATION

28. **Why is the term "goody-goody" a negative one? Isn't that a contradiction in terms?**
Society has given "good" and "goodness" a negative

connotation. Goodness is often not accepted for itself; it either means "self righteous" or a "holier than Thou" attitude.

What might provoke a person to refer to someone who does what is right as a "goody-goody"?
Possible answers: It may be that the person is unaccustomed to being around goodness. It may be a result of a perceived self righteous attitude on the part of the person who does what is right. It could be that the person is being convicted of sin.

33. What becomes of a tool that gets corroded with dirt or rust?
Its usefulness decreases or it becomes useless all together. It is no longer able to fulfill its purpose.

How does this relate to our usefulness to God as vessels of honor?
If we do not seek to do good in our lives, our usefulness decreases. We do not fulfill our purpose as God's workmanship: to perform good works in Christ.

KELLER QUOTATION

 LIFE SITUATION
Guy knew his friend Shel was having a hard time. His dad had been out of work for months, and he had been working until all hours of the night at his after-school job just to scrape enough money together to pay for his graduation pictures and the first semester of junior college. But Shel never complained and he never asked anyone for help. Guy knew Shel wouldn't want him, or anyone else, to know how hard his financial situation had been. So Guy took $150 out of his savings account and went by the portrait studio where Shel's graduation pictures were waiting to be paid for and picked up. When he handed the photographer the $150 in cash to pay for Shel's pictures, the photographer looked at Guy, whom he did not know, curiously. "I'm just a friend of Shel's. Don't mention it, OK?"

Though we can't know the intention of Guy's heart, what aspects of Christlikeness do you see in what he did?
He paid for Shel's pictures anonymously, and therefore received no personal gain or the gratitude or praise of his friend. He did not want to make Shel feel obligated or embarrass him on account of his deed. All he wanted to do was help his friend out in his time of need.

36. What kind of an effect do you think Guy's act of kindness would have on Shel in this situation?
Possible answers: It is possible that it would have no outward effect, but it is also possible that he would be intrigued by what would cause a person to act so selflessly on his behalf. It could create a hunger in him to seek out Christ. It could provide an opportunity for Guy to witness to him.

DAY 5

 FOCUS
We must treat others as we would like to be treated. When we limit our patience, kindness, and goodness to those who extend the same to us, we are generating those qualities from within ourselves. When we are able to extend patience, kindness, and goodness to those who are our enemies, it is a manifestation of the Holy Spirit within us.

APPLICATION
42. In what way is each of these statements faulty?
"I'm just treating him the way he deserves to be treated."
If we only treated others the way they deserved to be treated, there would be no forgiveness. Everyone would be treated badly because everyone fails. It would be a vicious cycle and we would never rise above it.
"I'm not going to break my back to help her out when she won't appreciate it anyway."
We should not be seeking the approval of men. We should only be seeking the approval of God.
"I am always sticking my neck out for her and she never does anything like that for me."
If this is the case, then the motive for doing good must be to eventually gain from it in some way.

44. When our actions toward others require us to overlook their actions, of whom are we a reflection?
We are a reflection of Christ. He overlooks our actions and blesses us in spite of them.

45. Why can we thank God for allowing our enemies to be a part of our lives?
It gives us the opportunity to experience the kind of patience, kindness, and goodness that originates from the Holy Spirit.

How much is your money worth?

WEEK 19
THE LOVE OF MONEY

 INTRODUCTORY ACTIVITY

Leader instructions:
Bring to the session a dollar bill of a large denomination, $50 or $100, if possible. Show the bill to the students and then fold it into a paper airplane. Fly the airplane through the air, letting it land where it may.

 DISCUSSION

What are you tempted to do?
Most students would admit to being tempted to snatch up the bill and keep it.

What do you think would happen if you were told that the first person to grab the bill would get to keep it?
Everyone would probably fight to get it.

What do you think would happen if we just left the bill on the floor during our discussion?
Possible answers: You would find yourself thinking about it periodically. It would make you feel uncomfortable to know that a large bill was just lying on the floor. You might even discover your mind wandering about what you would do with the money if you could keep it.

What do you think would be going through the mind of the person to whom the bill belonged?
Possible answers: He or she would probably desperately want to pick it up and put it away. He or she would worry about losing it. He or she might find him or herself thinking about it during the discussion.

Why do you think the bill brings out the emotions that it does from everyone involved?
Possible answers: It is an indication that we put too much emphasis and importance on money. We live in a materialistic society and therefore desire the money for what it can buy for us. It is an indication of the hold money has over us.

DAY 1

 FOCUS

While people are concerned with what they have, God is concerned with who they are. When a person loves money, he or she will not have a right relationship with the Lord because it is impossible to serve two masters. When your character is free from the love of money, you are free to trust in the Lord and place the priority on storing up eternal treasures rather than temporal ones.

APPLICATION

1. When we think in terms of a godly character, we may focus on areas such as patience, humility, kindness, etc. Why do you think we tend to minimize the love of money, seeing it as an insignificant characteristic that hampers godliness?
Possible answers: We see money and its acquisition as necessary in order to survive. We see it as relatively harmless compared to big sins such as cheating, lying, or murder. We can justify the acquisition of money based on the good we can do with it.

3. Although God does not promise to make us rich, what does He promise us in terms of our life on earth?
He does promise to meet our needs (Phil. 4:19).

4. Although it is possible to openly and blatantly reject God and His precepts in favor of pursuing riches, how can rejecting the Lord because of the love of money actually be something of which a person is not necessarily aware?
As your time becomes more and more consumed with obtaining wealth, your thoughts and actions become less centered on God and the things of His kingdom. You may discover that the time you once spent in prayer, for example, is now being spent working overtime at time-and-a-half.

5. When money is the master, obtaining it is the most important thing. Money as master demands that you obtain riches, and the end justifies the means. How does this open the door to compromise, affecting your entire character?

It may start with, for example, lying to a police officer about why you were speeding in order to avoid having to pay for a speeding ticket. A boss at a part-time job may ask you to lie or compromise for the sake of a dollar, and you oblige. You may decide to lie about your income in order to receive government help.

1 Corinthians 10:12
How might your character change over time if you suddenly inherited a great deal of money?

Possible answers: You might begin to place more and more importance on material things. As you obtain something you always wanted to have, you will inevitably want to obtain more. You might shun your less fortunate friends in favor of those who are able to afford the same extravagances you could now afford. You could neglect studying or working because making money is no longer a necessity, and you become lazy and self-absorbed.

DAY 2

FOCUS

While we may weary ourselves trying to obtain it, the reality of wealth is that it is unpredictable, unreliable, temporary, and fleeting. Those who love it put their trust in it because they look to it to meet the needs only God can meet, such as security, freedom, and happiness. Those who love money will not be satisfied with it, while those who love God will be satisfied with Him.

APPLICATION

10. Obviously, when you die you can't take the money you have worked so hard for with you. But what other ways could money make itself wings and fly away, at any given moment?

Possible answers: Money could be stolen. Jobs that pay high salaries could be lost. An unexpected illness could cause a person to lose his or her life savings.

How does God, as a master, compare to riches, as a master?

While riches are unpredictable, temporal, and fleeting, God is constant. He never leaves, never changes, and is eternal.

How does our attitude about winning a shopping spree to our favorite department store compare to our attitude about spending time with God? What do you think is the solution?

Unfortunately, we are usually more enthusiastic about obtaining temporal pleasures than we are with storing up eternal ones. The best solution to this problem is to have the self-discipline to avoid materialism and worldliness and to seek God, even when our emotions dictate otherwise. As we obey Him, our priorities will inevitably be affected.

11. You don't have to be wealthy to be concerned about money. Being able to pay for college, for example, is a primary concern for many youth. You may have no idea where the money will come from. Is it the money that will meet your need?

It is not the money that meets your needs. God meets your needs through such things as money. Therefore, we should trust in God and not in money and focus our time on growing closer to Him.

How do those who are not rich become slaves to material possessions?

They get into debt. They struggle, work, and weary themselves to pay back the money they have borrowed, plus the interest that has built up. Credit card debt is a very easy trap to fall into. You can have what you want now but pay for it later.

13. When we attribute to money the ability to provide security, freedom, happiness, and self worth, we look at it as though it had what nature?

We look at money as though it had the nature of God. He is the only one who can provide for those needs.

15. Psalm 4:7-8: How might people rely on money to provide them with safety? How successful will they be?

Possible answers: They might invest in sophisticated security systems, bulletproof glass, or body guards. Money cannot provide the kind of safety that knowing God can provide because there are aspects to life over which we can never have control. God, however, has control over all.

Psalm 145:19: What happens if we cry out to money to save us?

It can't save us. Although a person can "sell" his or her soul in many ways, he or she can never buy it.

DAY 3

FOCUS

When people place their trust in wealth, they often lose sight of their need for God, yet in so doing, they will perish. God is the giver of all wealth and the ability to make it, and we are its recipients only by grace. Just as God has generously shared His resources of wealth with us, so we too must model His example and extend generosity to others.

APPLICATION

16. What has a person who is self-made been given that has enabled him or her to possess wealth?
Possible answers: opportunities, intelligence, education, etc. He or she has been given everything, every circumstance, that enabled him or her to obtain wealth.

22. Should we give to others only if. . .
...we have anything left over?
...they deserve it?
...they appreciate our sacrifice?
...it doesn't force us to do without any of our own basic needs?
...they will do the same for us when we have a need?
We should give generously to others with pure motives regardless of our means or their response. This is the model of giving that Jesus demonstrated.

What is the only way to be purely motivated and generous in our giving?
The only way to do this is to have the proper perspective when it comes to money. We must view earthly riches in the same way that Jesus regarded them: as having little value. The real value lies in the riches of heaven.

DAY 4

FOCUS

In Luke 12, Jesus tells the story of the man who obtained great earthly wealth but had made no provision for eternity. His greed prevented him from even realizing his real need. Our attitude toward money is an indication of our spiritual state of being. For where our treasure is, there will our heart be also.

APPLICATION

LIFE SITUATION

24. There was no doubt about it: Ross had definitely lived a privileged life. His parents owned and ran their own corporation, and had enjoyed great financial success since before Ross was born. Although for the most part he had not been spoiled with material things, he had been given many material possessions that others only dreamed about. He always had money to spend. He always wore expensive clothes. For his sixteenth birthday, he had received a brand new sports car, and there were rumors that his parents would be treating him to a trip around the world for a graduation gift.

College, of course, was in his future. His parents could afford to send him wherever he wanted to go. With graduation just around the corner, he really felt that he would need a better form of transportation when he went to college. His car was nearly two years old, and he had his eye on a real beauty that he planned to mention to his parents.

Ross had heard his parents talking for several months about problems with the company. Tax problems, he thought they had said. He had paid little attention until the dreaded day when his parents sat him down to tell him that they were going to be forced to liquidate most of their assets in order to pay their tax debts. This included his car and much of his college fund. Not only could he forget about the real beauty he had his eye on, but he would even have to sell the car he had and settle for a basic, older model. And living at home while attending a local junior college was not exactly Ross's idea of striking out on his own, college life, big man on campus.

Ross knew his parents were devastated by their turn of fortune and he knew he should be supportive. But why did their misfortune have to totally screw up his life? After all, he was pretty sure they gave a lot of money to the church, and he had always been generous to others. Treating his friends to lunch was a common thing for him. He even tithed the allowance his parents gave him each week. Couldn't they have done something to keep this from happening? Didn't God care that his plans for the future were wrecked? Why didn't God honor Ross' faithfulness in giving? Why had God allowed this tragedy to happen at all?

How had Ross' wealth made him susceptible to greed?
He was no longer satisfied with the extravagant possessions he already owned. His two-year-old sports car was no longer good enough for him. Often, those who have much require still more in order to attempt to find contentment.

To whom is Ross' anger directed?
His anger is partly directed to his parents, but it seems to be directed more toward God.

What does Ross obviously not understand at this point in his life regarding wealth?
Ross does not realize that his family's wealth was a gift from God in the first place, and not anything they deserved or had earned without the benefit of God's intervention.

How could Ross allow the Lord to truly work in his life as a result of this situation?
Instead of being angry with God, he could determine to seek Him in the midst of this unexpected and difficult situation. He could learn to put his trust in God alone and never again in fleeting riches. God could teach Ross a great deal about meeting his needs if Ross is receptive and willing to learn.

27. How do you know you will be faithful to the Lord in giving to Him out of your wealth?
You will be faithful in giving to Him out of your wealth if you have been faithful to give to Him out of your poverty.

28. Anything that demands our undivided loyalty, forcing us to take our focus off of God, will create problems and anxieties for us. Think about people who are obsessed with wealth, deriving all of their security from it. To what problems does this often lead?
People whose trust is in their riches first become invincible. Nothing can hurt them because they have wealth, and with wealth comes power. Although they may think their money can take care of all of their problems, their lives and relationships are often in chaos. Suspicion becomes an issue. Are people only kind to them because of what they think they will get in return? They become competitive, not wanting to be outdone by others. The more material possessions others are able to afford, the more they will "need" as well in order to keep up. They may be overcome with the fear of losing their wealth.

DAY 5

 **FOCUS**
Greed is an easy trap for Christians to fall into because we can justify our desire for wealth by the good we will be able to do with it. Loving money is the root of every kind of evil.

APPLICATION
36. Can you think of examples where the love of money is the root of a particular evil in society?
Possible answers: the love of money is the cause of drug trafficking, gambling, prostitution, blackmail, kidnaping, robbery, embezzlement.

37. According to 1 Timothy 6:17, there can be some joy in riches. When do you think real joy in riches is possible?
It is only possible when a person has the proper perspective regarding money and material possessions, when he or she does not put any trust in them, and when God is the real source of joy in the person's life.

41. Why might God choose to bless a person financially, according to 1 Timothy 6:18?
He may give a person wealth so that he or she is able to give much to others. In this way, the person seeks riches in the body of Christ, which is where the longing of Christians should be.

42. When a person is given something that could only be given by God and is not a result of any act on his or her part, the joy is the greatest. For example, parents who are blessed with a child receive a gift that obviously could only be created and given to them by God. When we begin to view all of our possessions as gifts from Him, how will we begin to view them?
We will begin to appreciate them more and be grateful for what we have instead of longing for what we don't have.

44. When you see your ungodly peers who have many material possessions while you, who strive for godliness, have much less, what truths could you hold to when you are tempted to question God or see yourself as more deserving than they?
Nobody deserves any material possessions. Everything we have has been given to us through God's grace. We may not have the wealth that others possess, but we have the Source of all wealth in our lives and eternal rewards waiting for us.

DISCUSSION

Directions to leader:

The following discussion questions should be asked at the beginning of the study on contentment, and then discussed again at the conclusion of the study.

Once you begin a career, how much money do you think you would have to make in order to be content?

What would your spouse have to be like in order for you to be content in your marriage?

What kind of home would you need to own in order to be content living in it, and what type of vehicle would you need to drive in order to be satisfied?

Based on your answers, do you think your expectations and standards for contentment are high, average, or low?

DAY 1

FOCUS

The apostle Paul learned to be content regardless of his circumstances, even in the midst of hunger, thirst, and bitter persecution. While we often put our efforts into outside sources, thinking we will find contentment in them, real contentment is a result of seeking the Lord. He is contentment's only source.

APPLICATION

2. What is your level of contentment when you are hungry? Thirsty? Wearing a hand-me-down? Rejected by a friend? Treated unfairly?
Most people would have to admit that when circumstances make them uncomfortable or don't live up to their expectations, they experience discontentment.

3. Knowing that Paul was content even in the midst of beatings, stonings, and imprisonment, how do you feel about your own discontentment in the areas you listed on question number one in the student book?
Possible answers: The areas in which we experience discontentment are usually very minor compared to the things Paul endured while remaining content.

4. We look for everything on the outside to fill up the inside and make us content. How was Paul different?
Even in his complete emptiness, he had been filled with something.

5. What would have been the result if the secret Paul had learned was to put his energy into changing his situation? What can you learn from this?
If that had been his secret, he never would have found contentment. We often put all of our energy into trying to change our circumstances, many of which we have no control over. Therefore, contentment must lie in something other than ourselves and our circumstances.

7. What must be the goal of the person seeking contentment? Is it money? Fame? A number of satisfying relationships?
The goal is to know God, because that is where we will find contentment.

10. What happens if you sit in the same place for a long period of time?
You start to get uncomfortable. Your muscles may even start to cramp and tingle until you are no longer content to sit.

Are the following statements made by contented Christians?

"I am perfectly happy to believe in God and worship Him my way. I don't need organized religion."
"Even though my parents don't approve, I moved in with my boyfriend and I've never been happier."
"I'm content to be around my Christian friends. Let someone else go witness to those heathens."

These statements are made out of a false peace based on ignorance. Because the speakers aren't truly seeking God, they aren't going to find contentment, regardless of how satisfied they are with their circumstances.

DAY 2

 FOCUS

Godliness is a means of great spiritual gain when it's accompanied by contentment. Christians communicate that godliness is a burden when they are not content in it. Rather than pursuing earthly gain, we must spend our time and energy in the pursuit of knowing God.

 APPLICATION

11. What gain does each line of thinking suggest godliness will bring?
a. "I'll be too tired to study for my test after the church retreat. I don't know the stuff, but I'm sure God will help me do OK on it."
b. "Surely I can beat Jenna out for president. I mean, I'm a good girl and she has practically no morals at all."
c. "Why wouldn't God get me a good job after I graduate? I always tithe my money."
d. "They just have to choose me to get that scholarship. I do lots of community work through the church. No one else can say that."
Answers: a. a good grade; b. an elected office; c. money; d. an award

When we begin to think godliness will result in earthly rewards that serve to satisfy the flesh, what may become the purpose of our godliness?
It may be motivated by its perceived bargaining power: "Lord, if you will do this, I will. . ." This kind of gain is obviously not what Paul was referring to in 1 Timothy 6:6.

12. Indicate which of the following are forms of gain that accompany contentment:
a. joy
b. peace
c. quality relationships
d. a good reputation
e. happiness
f. security
g. eternal treasures
h a godly mate
i. fair treatment in the long run
j. remaining unaffected by negative circumstances; being free from the world
(Answers: a, b, e, f, g, j)

LIFE SITUATION

15. "So what I don't understand is why she thinks she has to walk the straight and narrow anyway," said Gina, who sometimes lost her patience with her friend, Kyla. Kyla just always seemed to be too busy with her church activities to spend time doing more fun things with her, and Gina was getting tired of it. It made her feel better to get it off her chest by complaining about Kyla to her friends in gym class.

"Yeah, really," said Payne. "It's probably just because her parents are so stuffy. I mean, don't they make her go to church all the time and stuff?"

"Well, she always seems to be there and I don't think she likes it too much," Rahim added.

"Well, all I know is, I could handle Kyla being such a goody-goody if she just didn't act so mad every time somebody gets something she doesn't have," said Gina. "I don't think getting mad a lot is good. It's like when my mom gave me $50 for my good grades, Kyla would hardly talk to me. I just don't get her."

Kyla may be pursuing godliness, but what is she communicating about it to her friends?
She is communicating that it does not satisfy. She may do what is right, but she is not content in it.

How do we know Kyla isn't content in striving toward godliness?
She is interested in material gain, is jealous of others, and may give her friends the impression that godliness is more of a burden than it is a path to contentment.

20. When you go to visit a relative for a few days, such as a grandparent, what do you expect to receive while you are there?
You probably expect food and shelter.

Why don't you expect to get a new car or a diamond ring while visiting your grandparents?
You see your visit as temporary.

When we put our energy and thoughts into obtaining material possessions, what kind of a mentality are we demonstrating?
We are demonstrating a permanent residence mentality. Yet according to James 4:14, we are just a vapor that appears for a little while and then vanishes away.

In what ways can we pursue contentment?
Possible answers: by not placing ourselves in situations where we are tempted to lack contentment, by seeking God, by doing without things we don't necessarily need, by giving to others in the midst of our own need.

DAY 3

 ## FOCUS

Paul was afflicted but not crushed, perplexed but not despairing, persecuted but not forsaken, struck down but not destroyed. His life is evidence to the fact that our contentment is not dependent on our circumstances, but instead is based on our source of strength. Jesus was attacked but did not attack in return. The same endurance and contentment He demonstrated is perfected in us today. If we submit to His Lordship, He will give us the contentment that can only come from knowing Him.

APPLICATION

21. The results of a fire or flood are outwardly obvious to any observer, but the results of affliction and persecution are not always so obvious. A person who is in the midst of a flood or fire is in immediate danger of losing his or her life, while this is not the case when he or she is afflicted, perplexed, persecuted, and struck down. Yet God said He would be with us and rescue us in the life-threatening trials. What does that say about our source of strength in times of persecution?
God must be our source of strength when we are afflicted, perplexed, persecuted, and struck down. If He will save us from the flames and the waters, He will surely rescue us from personal trials if we call on Him. And His grace is sufficient for us because His power is perfected in our weakness. (2 Cor. 12:9).

23. What do we know about the nature of God that allows us to remain above our circumstances, even when they seem to be the bleakest?
Because God is in control of our future, He knows what is best for us in the present and what our future holds, while we do not. We can trust Him.

25. We tend to tell ourselves that our level of contentment is based on our circumstances. If we just had that new car, we would be happy. If we just had a girlfriend or boyfriend, we would be satisfied. But what is the reality of the level of contentment we achieve when we obtain those things?
We may be happy with a new car for a while, but in a couple of years when it has a ding or two in it and has lost that new car smell, we are no longer content. We need a newer model. That girlfriend or boyfriend soon begins to show us his or her faults, and he or she may cause more grief than happiness in the long run. Our own experience should teach us that contentment does not lie in what we have.

27. We've all heard the expression, "When life gives you lemons, make lemonade." It means to make something good come out of a bad situation. It means to not let our circumstances get the best of us, regardless of what they are. But how can we possibly remain content when. . .
...our boyfriend/girlfriend breaks up with us and starts dating our best friend?
...the promise of getting an athletic scholarship is crushed in a single moment of injury?
...we suffer verbal and emotional abuse at home on a daily basis?
The only way to be unscathed by our circumstances is to submit to the Lordship of Christ, because contentment in such circumstances can only be a result of divine intervention. We must focus on God's promise in 2 Corinthians 4:17-18: "For momentary, light affliction is producing for us an eternal weight of glory far beyond all comparison, while we look not at the things which are seen, but at the things which are not seen; for the things which are seen are temporal, but the things which are not seen are eternal." We certainly will not find the strength to go on through years of therapy. We can only draw it from the Life Source.

DAY 4

 ## FOCUS

One of the most difficult areas in which we are able to find contentment is within our own persons. But God has created each of us in a special and unique way and for a specific purpose. We were created in His image and can be content in His lovingkindness.

APPLICATION

30. You may wish you could be taller or shorter, a little more outgoing instead of sometimes being too shy. Some aspects of ourselves cannot be changed because they are the result of the way God made us:

uniquely. We must be content in these areas. But in what areas of our lives should we never be content? We should never be content in our sin. For example, if we are prone to gossip about others, we can't use the excuse that it is just another aspect of our personality over which we have no control. We always have control over sin and we cannot be Christlike if we are comfortable in it.

33. An artist puts the thought, time, and care into making each painting or sculpture unique. The way God created us can be compared to an artist's painting, but it can also be compared to anything that shows careful, thoughtful planning, skill, and expertise. How, for example, can God's creation of each individual be compared to the making of a home-cooked meal rather than that of a TV dinner?
People who put together TV dinners do so in an assembly-line fashion. Every dinner is exactly like every other dinner, from cooking time to packaging. The people putting the dinners together are not thinking about who the meal is being prepared for. God did not create us to be like TV dinners. Instead, we are more like home-cooked meals. Each one is unique, planned, and prepared in a special, loving manner. A home-cooked meal consists of a variety of dishes and flavors, with just the right spices. Just as the cook tries to please those for whom he or she is preparing the meal by making dishes they enjoy, God fashions us not just for ourselves, but He considers those with whom we will come into contact, those our lives will affect. He created us the way we are not just for ourselves, but for others as well.

Think of another analogy that would compare something in our lives with the unique manner in which God created us. Share your thoughts with the group.

LUCADO QUOTATION
Think of something you have accomplished or made of which you are the most proud. How is it that God can put you in that same category: His creation of which He is the most proud?
Because when He sees us, He sees His Son who is in us.

36. Why should we be grateful for our imperfections?
If we had no physical imperfections, for example, we might be tempted to put our trust in our looks rather than in God. Imperfections create in us the need to seek out perfection in something other than ourselves.

DAY 5

 FOCUS

In the face of complete destitution, Habakkuk was able to rejoice in the Lord. Our contentment is not threatened in the face of despair when our strength comes from God. Only the Lord puts gladness in our hearts that transcends any earthly material blessing.

 APPLICATION

42. In these verses, the psalmist does not question God, but is humble in the face of tribulation. Why is it so important that we not mull over things that happen in life that we do not understand?
It is not the humble who think they can come up with answers to questions that are beyond themselves. We do not have the mind of God. We must leave the things we do not understand to God, knowing that He does have all of the answers. "Behold, I am the Lord, the God of all flesh; is anything too difficult for Me?" Jeremiah 32:27. Our problems are no match for God.

What image comes to mind when you think of a small child resting against his or her mother (Psalm 131:2)?
It is the picture of complete security. No matter what happens, he or she relies on his or her mother to take care of everything. We can have this same confidence in God and rest in His answers.

45. Instead of wishing for things we think will make us happy and keep us content, all we really need to ask of the Lord is what?
We need only to ask that He will put gladness and contentment in our hearts, regardless of our blessings or perceived lack of them.

DISCUSSION

Ask the same four discussion questions found at the beginning of this session.

After completing the study, students should realize that their contentment does not lie in how much money they are someday able to make, their career choices, their future spouse, or any material possession. The only thing that will enable them to be content is their relationship with God, and knowing and trusting Him.

WEEK 21
ANXIETY

DAY 1

 FOCUS

God, who provides for the birds of the air and the lilies and the grass of the field, is faithful to supply all of our needs as well. Anxiety is a result of a lack of trust in God and others. Worry is doubting the very character of God. When we do not trust Him, it is a result of focusing on our needs rather than on Him. As we seek Him, He will provide.

 APPLICATION

7. We don't give a great deal of thought to the provisions God makes for the birds or the flowers. We aren't concerned about their well-being because we take for granted the fact that they have everything they need, that God is providing for them. What can we learn from this in terms of our own lives?
Instead of being anxious for our provisions, we must know that God will provide for us. He doesn't require or need our anxiety before He will act, but He does require our faith.

8. While faith moves mountains, what does anxiety accomplish?
Anxiety actually creates its own mountains.

11. When we choose to worry, we choose to be in control. We take our problems to worry instead of to God. In this situation, of what are we guilty?
We are guilty of idolatry. Anything we run to in times of trouble other than God is an idol.

We can do many things without faith: we can make good grades, get married, and start a career. But we cannot please God when we worry because we're demonstrating a lack of faith in Him. When we worry, whose voice are we choosing to listen to?
We are listening to the voice of Satan who says, "Things can't possibly work out," and "You can't see it, so it must not be real."

CHAMBERS QUOTATION
How can we be certain that God will supply our needs?
It is God's very nature to be faithful, and His nature does not change. Second Timothy 2:13 says, "If we are faithless, He remains faithful; for He cannot deny Himself."

12. When our focus is on Christ, and He is first in our lives, how do you think it will impact our anxieties?
When Christ is first, we will have the right perspective on everything else. As we seek Him, trust Him, and see the results, we will learn to trust Him even more. When we worry, our focus isn't on Him.

We must trust Him and keep our focus on who He is and what He provides. When we worry, our focus, instead, is on what?
Worry is a result of focusing on what is missing or lacking in our lives rather than on what God supplies. In this case, our trust is in what we have, and our anxieties are rooted in our lack.

DAY 2

 FOCUS

Natural disasters, international tragedies, and world issues are areas that could create anxiety in our lives, yet God tells us in His Word that He is in control of them and is our stronghold in the midst of them. When we find ourselves feeling anxious, we must be still and listen to God, shutting out the noise of the world and seeking only His direction.

 APPLICATION

15. Why is worrying about the "what if's" a unique form of anxiety?
Worrying about "what if's" is actively seeking out areas of anxiety.

GRIFFITH QUOTATION
Describe characteristics of truly anxious people.
Possible answers: Anxious people seem nervous much of the time. They could even be known to say such things as, "I'm worried about something, but I don't know what it is." They often assume the worst in any given situation. If they hear a siren, for example, someone they know and love must have been involved in an accident. They could be doom seekers who worry when there is nothing to be anxious about. When things are going well, they think something must be about to go wrong. They do not ever seem to experience the peace God has to offer them because they are unwilling to turn their anxieties over to Him.

20. Why could anxieties regarding natural disasters, international tragedies, and other world issues all be considered "what if" worries?
They are things over which we have absolutely no control and many times they are things which have little probability of happening.

 LIFE SITUATION
23. Neil felt the walls closing in on him. He had been mad at his mom for making him watch his little brother. "Nathan is such a pain," Neil had thought. "He's not my responsibility!" If only his attitude had been different and he had been watching him more closely, then he could have yelled at Nathan before he rode his bicycle out into the middle of the street without looking both ways. Now they were in the emergency room, and Nathan was lucky to only have a broken leg and a few cracked ribs.

Neil's parents would be furious with him. They would blame him for Nathan's accident. He's just a little kid, after all. They would never forgive him. He could see the look of scorn that would be meant for him and hear their cutting words. They would probably make him get a job to pay for the emergency room bills. Forget about playing tennis in the spring. Forget about the prom or graduation parties. He would be paying for this for the rest of his life.

What do you think is fueling Neil's anxieties?
Part of his anxiety could be due to feelings of guilt.

How could Neil benefit from being still and ceasing his striving?
If Neil shut out all of his anxieties, those that are fueled by real circumstances as well as those that are likely to be imagined, and shifted his focus to God

and what He has to say to Him, he would find great comfort, direction, and guidance in this situation.

How could Neil go about seeking God's direction?
He could spend the energy he has used in worry to pray for his brother, his parents, the driver of the car that hit Nathan, and the circumstances he now finds himself in. He could seek God, His leadership, and His comfort. He could benefit greatly from spending time in God's Word.

DAY 3

 FOCUS
When in the presence of Christ, the father of a demon-possessed boy was able to trust God to cast out the source of his years of anxiety. It was not the man's endurance or concern that caused Jesus to act. It was his faith. We do not demonstrate our concern for the trials of others by worrying about them. Instead, we demonstrate our concern when we pray and seek the Lord's guidance, leaving the burdens and the results to Him.

APPLICATION
24. This event, where Jesus was confronted with a demon-possessed boy, directly follows the transfiguration, when Jesus took Peter, James, and John up into the mountain and affirmed His deity. What is the significance that the disciples were taken from the edge of heaven to the pit of hell in such a brief period of time? How does this relate to our anxiety?
Anxiety is doubting and even denying God and His power. Faith and trust in Him are a result of listening to His voice above all others. Giving in to anxiety and rising above it are as contrasting as the difference between the experience of heaven and the reality of hell. It is belief versus unbelief.

27. Worry is not just something negative in and of itself. It has the potential to multiply and overpower. What other aspects of the father's feelings regarding his son's ordeal do you think were a result of his anxiety?
Possible answers: helplessness, despair, sadness, weariness, desperation, anger, embarrassment, etc.

28. How might the man's actions through the years have contributed to his lack of faith?
Because nothing had worked, he probably was desperate for someone, anyone, to give him an answer.

32. So often we come to God in our times of desperation on our terms. What does Jesus' response to the people indicate is His attitude regarding this line of thinking?

It angers Him. We must come to God on His terms, and this means in complete faith and trust in whom He is and in His sovereignty.

34. What do you think is the significance in the fact that once the demon was driven out, the boy was as still as a corpse?

It is the enemy that keeps us agitated, that keeps us stirred up, that keeps us striving and anxious. Once the enemy is defeated, there is rest.

DAY 4

 FOCUS

Just as not all of the Israelites who were led out of Egypt made it to the promised land of Canaan because of their unbelief and disobedience, not all Christians enter the Lord's rest for the same reasons. Entering His rest is the goal of Christians: to experience the calm, confident, victorious peace that is the very nature of God. Anxiety is the evidence of a disobedient life, and therefore prevents such rest.

 APPLICATION

40. Why is it that Christians do not necessarily enter into the Lord's rest?

It is the same reason that not all of the Israelites entered into Canaan—disobedience and unbelief. We cannot expect to be free from the worries of the world and receive the peace of God that passes all understanding if we are not willing to obey and trust Him.

45. If you are experiencing anxiety in your life, it is likely to be a result of disobedience or a lack of trust in God. If you are listening to the Spirit's voice, what are examples of things He might be convicting you of that would enable you to get to the root of your anxiety?

Possible answers: areas of your life in which you are not trusting God, relationships that exist in your life that should be changed, mended, or eliminated, the state of your thought life, your use of words that may discourage and tear down rather than encourage and uplift, etc.

DAY 5

 FOCUS

Our sin hinders us from the goal of resting in the Lord. David learned the secret of peace in any circumstance: seeking God above all else. When we make Christ Lord of our lives and cast our burdens on Him, He sustains us with His strength and peace.

 APPLICATION

47. Can you experience God's rest in your life if you....
...gossip about others?
...are reluctant to inconvenience yourself in order to help someone else?
...worry about what others think or say about you when you aren't around?
...pray without any real expectation that your prayers will be answered?
...have a bad attitude toward parental authority?
...choose to associate with peers who could be described as a bad influence?
...are afraid of the future?

God's rest cannot be experienced when you harbor sin in your life.

50. Through what "extreme" circumstances in your life would you like to find contentment?

Answers will vary. Students may choose to share difficult trials they are currently experiencing in which they are seeking contentment.

Verse 4 holds the key. . .
What do you think will happen in a world of uncertainty and insecurity if we choose to seek just Him?

If we are truly seeking just the Lord, we will inevitably discover that we can be content regardless of our circumstances and we can experience the peace and rest He intended for us to have in Him.

55. How do you think you will know when you have truly cast your burdens on the Lord and are trusting in Him?

You will no longer worry about them.

WEEK 22
JOY AND PEACE

DAY 1

FOCUS

The true Christian experience lies in righteousness, joy, and peace in the Holy Spirit. Rule-keeping can never create peace within us. Instead, God fills us with His joy and peace when we accept Christ as our Savior, but we must make ourselves available to Him in order to experience it.

APPLICATION

1. If you asked a non-Christian what it means to be a Christian, he or she might say such things as, "going to church on Sundays," or "reading your Bible," or "not doing really bad things." But in what way is the reality of the Christian experience summed up not in what we do, but rather in how we are able to live in a world of sin?

It is a matter of living above the world and its sin, choosing not to participate in it, and experiencing joy and peace in the midst of it.

2. When we put our confidence in our deeds, whose rules are we following?

We are following rules we have set up for ourselves, and not necessarily God's rules.

3. If our deeds could create lasting joy and peace, what would that say about God's love for us?

Then God's love for us would be conditional. He would grant us His joy and peace based on our performance rather than on His Son.

When we are saved, Christ enters our life and puts His fruit of joy and peace in our hearts. Does this mean we will always experience it?

No. We will not experience His joy and peace, for example, when we are participating in sin.

Joy is the real fruit of the Spirit. But sometimes what may appear to be joy isn't joy at all. What would be the artificial fruit that may look like joy, but in reality is only an inferior imitation?

Happiness is the artificial fruit because it is based solely on circumstances.

Describe the relationship between real fruit and artificial fruit and how that relates to Spirit-produced joy and mere circumstance-based happiness.

Real fruit can be eaten and is nourishment for the body. It looks pretty on the outside, and its smell and taste are pleasant to the senses. The true fruit of joy is not only pleasant in terms of experience, but it also nourishes the soul. It looks pretty to the outside world, and its effect is pleasing to the person who experiences it. Within the fruit is the seed, which is its very life. Within the fruit of joy is life, because it can only come from the Holy Spirit within us.

Artificial fruit cannot be eaten. It may look pretty on the outside and may even look real, but in it there is no nourishment, nothing pleasant in its taste or smell, and there is no life within it. Because it contains no real seeds, it is unable to reproduce itself. The artificial fruit of happiness looks pretty on the outside and gives the impression that it is full of life. It is not a result of the life of the Holy Spirit, but of the temporary circumstances of the moment.

5. Of all of the ways in which we can make ourselves accessible to God, which one is the key and why?

Prayer is the key because it sets the perspective for everything else in our life. We keep Christ in every situation and circumstance of our life when we pray without ceasing (1 Thessalonians 5:17).

DAY 2

FOCUS

Jesus promises us His inward joy that is present regardless of outward circumstances. Remaining in the presence of the Lord and knowing and doing His will allows His joy to be made full in our lives. Nothing that touches our lives can get closer to us than Christ who indwells us.

APPLICATION
Although Jesus faced persecution from every side, He experienced joy in the midst of it. What do you think enabled Jesus, the man, to experience such joy in spite of such oppression?
He was one with the Father.

7. How do you set the Lord continually before you. . .
...in your most difficult class?
...when someone "stabs you in the back"?
...when everyone around is using His name in vain?
...when someone you love dies tragically?
God is always accessible through prayer. Recalling Scripture, such as Colossians 1:17, "And He is before all things, and in Him all things hold together," enables us to meditate on His truths. Because Christ is in us, nothing can get closer to us than He can. The knowledge of this fact enables us to keep Him continually before us.

8. "If I could just make an A on this test, I would be ecstatic!"
"If she would go out with me, I would be the happiest person in the world."
"If my parents would just quit fighting all the time, I could truly be happy."
"When I finally get out of Mrs. Jones' biology class, I will be thrilled!"
How effective do you think the reality of these situations taking place will be in terms of the level of joy the speakers will experience?
A high test score, a date, a peaceful home environment, and getting out of an unpleasant or difficult situation might produce joy for a moment. But when the moment wears off or the circumstances change, something else is needed to provide happiness. There will be others tests, other dates, other problems, and other difficulties that will require solutions in order for happiness or joy to exist.

10. Sometimes we may be tempted to think that knowing and doing the will of God will be more stifling than good, that it will produce just the opposite of joy. What do you think contributes to this view?
Possible answers: Doing God's will means giving control over to Him when we would actually like to be the one in control. We may have a false concept of God, viewing Him, for example, like a parent who

wants to tell us what to do. We may think that His will couldn't possibly be the same as our will because it wouldn't be as exciting or because we would have to give up too much.

DAY 3

FOCUS
Happiness is not the same as joy because it is dependent on positive circumstances. The early Christians experienced joy in the midst of great tribulation. Circumstances can never produce joy because they change. Christ, who is the source of joy, never changes. We cannot experience joy when we choose sin because sin in our lives quenches the Spirit.

APPLICATION
13. Hebrews 10:34. When the early Christians had all of their earthly possessions taken from them, they rejoiced. How does this contradict the world's idea of joy?
The world sees joy in the accumulation of worldly possessions, but this demonstrates that real joy does not rest in material things.

1 Peter 1:6. What do you think is a reliable indication that joy is of the Spirit and not merely an imitation of the real fruit?
When there is joy in spite of and in the midst of trials, it can only be a result of the joy of God's Holy Spirit. James 1:2-4 says, "Consider it all joy, my brethren, when you encounter various trials, knowing that the testing of your faith produces endurance. And let endurance have its perfect result, that you may be perfect and complete, lacking in nothing."

HAMILTON QUOTATION
What are examples of things the world says will create happiness?
Possible answers: a satisfying career, a boyfriend/girlfriend, money and the things it can buy, getting good grades, loyal friends.

"And there is a difference between knowing how to laugh and knowing how to rejoice." When we see a person who is fun-loving and cheerful, we assume that he or she is a generally happy person. But why is it that in the absence of the indwelling of Christ, the person cannot truly be filled with joy?
While the world sees the outward countenance, the heart sees the other side of the mask. Proverbs

14:13 says, "Even in laughter the heart may be in pain, and the end of joy may be grief." A person who knows how to laugh when things are going well or when he or she is experiencing fun does not necessarily know how to experience joy when the going gets tough.

 ## LIFE SITUATION

14. Tamra was on the top of the world. Everyone was talking about how Dale, the best looking guy in the whole senior class, was crazy about her. There was a spring in her step and a smile on her face as she thought about where they would go when he asked her out. She liked the way people told her what a cute couple they would make. They would look so good together in their prom picture!

"Oh yeah, Dale's going to the prom," she walked up just in time to overhear Melissa say. "He just asked Melia this morning."

Before Tamra heard the rumors about Dale's interest in her, she was dateless and lonely. How do you think she felt once she heard about Dale's prom date?
She probably felt even worse: dateless, lonely, rejected, and maybe even stupid.

What happened to the spring in her step and the smile on her face?
They disappeared when her circumstances changed.

15. Why does the joy of the Lord never disappoint?
Because unlike our circumstances, the Lord never changes.

19. How is the relationship between joy and sin like the relationship between fire and water?
Just as water puts out a fire, sin quenches the Spirit and its fruit in our lives.

DAY 4

 ## FOCUS

The ministry of Jesus on earth began and ended with peace. He established the vertical peace between God and human beings through His death, as well as the horizontal peace among all of mankind. A person cannot experience peace outside of Christ. We must seek Him daily in order to experience the ongoing peace He intends for us.

 ## APPLICATION

23. What things come to mind when you think of the peace of the world?
Possible answers: It is incomplete, temporary, subject to change based on the situation.

24. Even in the best moments, the peace of the world is artificial. Why do you think this is the case?
The world hasn't made peace with God. When there is no peace vertically (in the cross) there can be no peace horizontally (among mankind).

A mother of two who left her husband to pursue a lesbian relationship with another woman was heard to say, "It was the best decision I ever made. I've never been happier in my life."

A woman who had been married several times before, and claimed she always married for love, said, "This one is a match made in heaven. It will last forever."

A teenager who enjoyed experimenting with drugs once told a counselor, "I love doing drugs. I mean, how can you feel bad about something that makes you feel so good?"

These speakers may fool themselves for a while, or they may just be attempting to fool others. How do we know that what they are saying are lies?
No matter where they might seek it, no matter how hard they try, there can be no peace for the wicked (Isaiah 57:21).

STANLEY QUOTATION
When we think of joy and peace, we think of emotion. But how do you think the joy and peace of Christ go beyond mere emotion?
They are more states of mind, states of being, than states of temporary emotion. Jesus is the source of joy and the author of peace. The difference could be compared to boiling water. The less water there is in the pot, the quicker it boils. The less substance that exists in a situation, the more we can get our emotions going. With Christ, the joy and peace are deeper. There is far more water in the pot.

30. John 16:33 promises us that we will have tribulation in the world. But what is our assurance when we look around and every indication tells us evil reigns?
The assurance is that Jesus has already overcome the world through His death, and that we, too, may

overcome evil with good in the world by the power of His Spirit within us (Romans 12:21).

OGILVIE QUOTATION
The peace of God does not sit passively by as we struggle with the world's obstacles. How does this quotation allude to the real power of peace?
Peace is a weapon. Like a sword that helps you bring down a foe, peace enables you to overcome evil.

DAY 5

FOCUS
We must outwardly show the Spirit's peace in our lives through our relationships with others. This means paying back good for evil and not using our thoughts or our words as tools of revenge. In doing so, we are giving them a picture of Christlikeness.

APPLICATION
31. What kind of excuses do we sometimes use to justify not pursuing peace with certain people?
Examples: "I can't just let him get away with the way he's treating everybody!" "She's got a problem with me and I haven't even done anything wrong!" "Why should I always have to be the one to give in, especially when I'm right?"

32. Although we may be tempted to take the situation into our own hands when someone is unjustifiably at war with us, what must we keep in mind in terms of the reality of the battle?
When someone we are trying to be at peace with is warring against us, we must realize that it is not a human battle, but it's a spiritual one. The only thing to do is to pray for the strength to be obedient and to love the person.

What was Christ's reaction to all of the people who were at war with Him?
He loved them, and He humbled and surrendered Himself not to them, but to God.

If you obey God and surrender your actions to Him and His will, then who is the battle between?
Then the battle is between the person and God.

33. What is accomplished when we pay back evil for evil?
The only thing accomplished is evil. There is no reconciliation, no resolution, and definitely no peace.

Returning evil for evil is a never-ending cycle that eventually leads to disaster.

According to Proverbs 12:20, if you want to experience joy in your life, what must you be seeking?
Peace with everyone.

39. Why is God's vengeance better than our own?
It is because God vindicates us in the process. He upholds His righteous ones.

LIFE SITUATION
Philippe knew Curtis had been stabbing him in the back. He was nice to him to his face most of the time, but that didn't stop Curtis from calling him every name in the book when Philippe wasn't around. Philippe was just beginning to realize why Keri had broken up with him with no explanation. She had been spending a lot of time with Curtis lately. There was no telling what Curtis had told her about him. Philippe couldn't bring himself to forgive and forget about all the times Curtis had taken advantage of him. And now Curtis had the nerve to ask Philippe to lend him $150 to pay for the dent he put in the fender of his mother's car!

"No more," Philippe told his friend Ahmud. "If I helped him out, I'd just be a hypocrite, 'cause I don't want to help him at all. I don't even like him and I'm tired of being insincere about it!"

If Philippe has the means to help Curtis and doesn't, is his hypocrite theory justifiable?
We cannot justify doing wrong or not doing right because it would be in conflict with our emotions. We are not being hypocritical to do the right thing, we are being obedient to God.

When you do good to those who do evil to you, and you feel like they are getting the best of you, what must you remember in terms of whom you must be seeking to please and from where the peace comes?
It is important to remember that you are doing good not to please the person, but rather to please God. Your peace does not rest in the person anyway. It rests in God and is a result of your obedience to Him.

"I don't feel like going to church this morning, so if I go, I'll just be a hypocrite."
What is wrong with this statement?
You are never being a hypocrite when you override your emotions in order to obey God.

WEEK 23
COURAGE

DAY 1

 FOCUS

Having courage is having the moral character that is rooted in the character of God. Leaving the Lord out of our challenges results in fear. Because God is the source of courage, when we fear Him, there is nothing else to fear.

 APPLICATION

1. From your observations, how would the world characterize a person who lacks courage?
Possible answers: weak, passive, insecure, etc.

LUCADO QUOTATION
What kind of exterior supports may temporarily sustain us in our pursuit of courage in our lives?
Possible answers: parents, positive peer influences, ministers and other leaders in the church.

OGILVIE QUOTATION
"This is going to be the hardest test I've ever taken. I just don't think I can do it," Josie thought as her heart began to pound.
"I'm afraid to stand up to Jay," said Kent. "If I tell him I won't help him cheat, I know he'll get even."
Gretta felt her throat go dry and her stomach tighten as her name was called. She found it difficult to catch her breath long enough to start the cheer she would be performing for tryouts.

What action do you think would benefit Josie, Kent, and Gretta in their fear-provoking situations?
They don't need to face their fears on their own, but should seek the Source of courage and strength.

Have you ever tried to battle fears such as these on your own? What was the result?
Possible answers: Attempting to battle your fears based on your own strength will be unsuccessful. No matter how hard you try to muster up courage on your own, you can't do it without going to its Source.

Based on verse 26, where does real strength lie?
Real strength lies in realizing that we all have a handicap, which is our flesh, and that apart from Christ we can do nothing (John 15:5).

Why is Christ so much more superior than a literal crutch or any other type of figurative crutch we might rely on for temporary strength?
A crutch is something that is outside of yourself, and is often a temporary solution. Crutches could be things besides Christ that we run to in times of fear, such as worry or alcohol. Christ is not outside of us, but rather He lives within us forever.

8. When we fear the Lord, does this mean that all of our other fears will never come to pass? Does it mean we will never fail, never be excluded, never be lonely, and never experience physical harm?
No. But it does mean God will replace our fear with His peace if we seek Him in the middle of it. He will never allow the righteous to be shaken (Ps. 55:22).

DAY 2

 FOCUS

Courage is power with love as its motive and discipline to hold it accountable. The world's greatest fear is a result of its spirit of sin, which leads to death. Through Christ, we have been set free from the fear of death and have been given power to overcome the evil one.

 APPLICATION

9. When we think of courage, we usually think of power, but we don't necessarily think of love. Power without love seeks its own; it takes control. What is the outcome of power with love?

Power with love is able to lift others up to God.

14. Discipline holds the power of courage accountable to love. What would power be like without love and discipline?
It would be self-seeking at the very least and cold-blooded at its worst. People all over the world have suffered great oppression at the hands of those who possessed great power in the absence of love and discipline.

DAY 3

 FOCUS

The twelve leaders sent by Moses to spy out the promised land persuaded the Israelites that they would be defeated in battle by the people in the land of Canaan. Because of their lack of faith in God, the people wandered in the wilderness for 40 years. We must guard against persuasive leaders and the voice of the majority, having the courage to follow the voice and direction of the minority, where we will find God.

APPLICATION

20. The leaders reported that the people were so big, they were like grasshoppers in comparison to them. This, of course, was an exaggeration, but we are often guilty of the same. Why do we tend to stack the odds against ourselves when we are faced with a difficult and intimidating situation?
When we exaggerate our disadvantage, it tends to explain and justify failure. It is a clear indication that we lack courage.

21. If the leaders had followed instructions and given a factual account of the land and the people, how do you think the Israelites might have responded?
They might have been concerned about the size of the people, but would not have considered themselves as defeated before the battle even began. It was the initial disobedience of the leaders that started the rebellion which ended in disaster.

What does this say about the voice of pessimism?
It is extremely persuasive.

22. What does Caleb's response tell you about His relationship with the Lord?
He saw what God told Him to see because his eyes were focused on the Lord.

 LIFE SITUATION

A. "I really don't think you should be looking at going on that mission trip this summer," Ramone's mother told him. "I know you'd like to do something like that, and you may even feel that's what God wants, but honey, we just don't have the money to send you."
B. "You can't seriously think that they would actually hire you for that job, Kyle!" Eva told him. "I've known you for a long time and I don't think you could handle it. You're not even that good at math."
C. "If I were you, I would pursue something a little, shall we say, less challenging," the school counselor told Alisha. "After all, pre-med is a hard major. Let's look at these brochures from some local community colleges."

The voice of pessimism can come from many sources: a friend, a parent, a teacher. Once we understand this, what should we keep in mind?
We should be seeking God's voice above all others. His is the voice of optimism, faith, love, and courage.

25. How did the reaction of the people toward Aaron and Moses go beyond rebellion?
They didn't just reject them, they hated their faith and wanted to destroy it.

27. Because a group of leaders determined, by their own wisdom, what would be the right thing to do, everyone else followed, and an entire nation was punished. How does this relate to your own life?
The leaders among youth are often those who follow the path of darkness. All who follow this path face punishment. Because the voice of the majority can be so persuasive, it takes great courage from God to stay true to His value system.

DAY 4

 FOCUS

The Lord commissioned Joshua to be strong and courageous in fighting the people of Canaan. Courage comes through careful obedience to God and His Word. If we are to have the courage to succeed in living according to God's will, we must be disciplined in our obedience to Him.

APPLICATION

36. You know without a doubt that God is commissioning you to go to a specific college. Your parents say they can't afford to send you. Your friends are

encouraging you to go to the same college they will be attending. Your counselor tells you your grades may not be good enough to get in. The odds seem stacked against you. Yet how do you find the courage to persist in your resolve to go where God leads?

Your courage shouldn't lie in the opinions of others or even in yourself. Your courage lies in God and His promises. He will finish what He starts and His presence and influence will be with you in your efforts to follow through.

37. When we are guilty of disobedience, we tend to isolate ourselves from God. We just don't want to face up to our sin. But when we isolate ourselves from God, we become vulnerable to Satan's voice. We begin to question everything we do in terms of whether we are now in line with God's will or if we have stepped out of it. How do we avoid such confusion?

When we fail, we must acknowledge our failures before God. We can get right back into line with His will because of His forgiveness, but we can't do it if we run from Him.

Why are our decisions not sound when we are giving in to sin?

Sound decisions come from a spirit of power and love and discipline (2 Timothy 1:7) which result from obeying God, and not from a spirit of timidity and weakness, which lead to disobedience.

DAY 5

FOCUS

The Lord used 300 faithful men to conquer the huge armies of the Amalekites and the Midianites. In reducing the numbers of the Israelites, they would be forced to rely on the Lord for their victory and He would be glorified in it. We must have the courage to trust in God in spite of the obstacles and, like the 300, persevere to the end.

APPLICATION

45. Imagine the conversations that could have gone on among the 22,000 men who returned home because they were afraid. What do you think they might have said about the 300 who were to fight?

Possible answers: "They will all be killed." "They're crazy to even try to fight." "They will make our whole nation look weak."

The world tries to turn morality around, saying those who do what is right are the uncool ones. With this in mind, what else do you think the 22,000 could have been saying in order to discredit the 300?

Possible answers: "Those goody-goodies, they think they're so important." "Can you believe the way they drink water?" or "They are dumber than sticks."

48. Can you think of a time in your life when you were definitely following the Lord in spite of the pessimism of those around you, and the Lord did something to affirm to you that what you were doing was right? Share your experience with the group.

52. The soldiers turned on each other and destroyed themselves. Do you notice the same thing happening today among those who, although in the majority, choose the path of sin?

Those who commit crimes end up in jail. Those who cheat in school end up getting caught and receive failing grades. Those who break the rules end up getting suspended. There is no peace for the wicked.

56. Why do you think the 300 still wanted to fight, even with such unconventional weapons?

Their confidence was not in their weapons. Their faith was in God.

Why do you think God might choose to strip us of our resources, seemingly making success more difficult to achieve?

When our trust in ourselves and our abilities is hampered, we are forced to rely fully on Him. And the glory for our successes will go to Him as well.

57. In terms of modern-day Christianity, the "32,000" are those who respond to the altar call. Twenty-two thousand of those, however, lose their faithfulness and fearing the rejection of the majority, quickly fall back into the patterns of worldliness. Who are the 300?

They are those who persevere until the end. They are the ones who have the courage to trust God, obey Him, and finish the race.

59. Ordinary courage receives its reward in the form of the praise and recognition of others. From where does the reward for the true hero come?

The true hero, who has the courage to persevere, is exalted by God.

WEEK 24
INTEGRITY

 DISCUSSION

When you think of people who have integrity, what characteristics come to mind?

Possible answers: living a godly life, having high moral standards, people who will do the right thing even when no one is watching.

Why do you think this standard is important in the pursuit of Christlikeness? Isn't it good enough just to be perceived as a "good person" by the world's standards?

Integrity involves going beyond what the world says is acceptable moral behavior. It is the behavior demonstrated by Jesus in all things. So, if we are to be like Him, we too must walk in integrity.

we still might fall short when it comes to matters of integrity. Why is this so?

It is one thing to know the truth but it is another thing to apply it to our lives through our daily lifestyle.

5. Do you think the psalmist's refusal to associate with the wicked was a result of self-righteousness?

It was not a result of self-righteousness, but rather a determination to avoid temptation. Associating with the wicked desensitizes us to sin.

8. If you are a person who truly enjoys worship and seeking Christ, what are you likely to be cultivating in your life?

You are likely to be becoming a person of integrity.

DAY 1

 FOCUS

It is our relationship with Christ that enables us to walk in integrity. We seek to honor Him through obedience to Him in all things, not merely in what can be seen by others or through living a life of acceptable morality by the world's standards. In order to become people of integrity, we must love worship and truly desire to seek Him.

 APPLICATION

3. Sometimes we can justify telling a "little white lie," thinking that no one will know. We may even think that if we don't confess our sin before God, we can keep it from Him as well. But what is the reality of such action?

The reality is that all things are before God's eyes. There is nowhere to hide, no way to pretend, and there are no false supports.

4. We may have attended church all of our lives. We may know the truths of the Lord. In fact, we may possess great Biblical and spiritual knowledge. Yet

DAY 2

 FOCUS

A person who walks in integrity lives righteously and speaks truth in his or her heart. A person of integrity, whose foundation is Christ, will never be shaken. Integrity prepares us for our eternal dwelling place because it conforms us to the image of Christ.

APPLICATION

12. "I might not return a small amount of change to the grocery store clerk who gave me back too much, but if it were say, over a dollar, I would do it."

"I might tell a little white lie if it didn't hurt anybody, but I would never tell a really big lie."

"I might confirm information about someone if it were true, but I would never spread a rumor."

"I might try to cheat on my taxes some day. After all, we do have to pay too much in taxes, don't we? But I would never cheat on a test or anything. That would be really wrong."

What is the reality of all of these statements?
These people are attempting to justify their "little" sins by refusing to commit what they see as "bigger" sins. It is an indication that they do not truly understand that all sin, "big" or "little," is the same in the sight of God. It is also an indication that they are not living lives of integrity.

13. Why do you think a person who possesses integrity will value that characteristic in others?
Possible answers: It means they share a common value system. Those traits that we find important in our own lives we will also consider to be important in the lives of others. It means that the person can be trusted.

DAY 3

FOCUS

As governor of Judah, Nehemiah chose to go against tradition and give of his own resources to the people rather than taxing them, and he worked with them in their labor. A person of integrity, like Nehemiah, will not be content to go along with the status quo, but instead will desire to seek and obey the commands of God. Taking a stand for what is right has the potential to affect many.

APPLICATION

21. It would have been easy for Nehemiah to justify conforming to the practices of former governors. How do we do the same thing in attempting to justify improper actions in our own lives?
We justify our actions based on the fact that "everyone else" does it. This is often used as the excuse for immorality, using alcohol, etc. If the action is improper but has been accepted for a long period of time, such as gossiping, it is easy to justify because no one seems to object.

MACLAREN QUOTATION

LIFE SITUATION

Jaren sat on his bed thinking about the big party he would be going to in a few hours. Some of his friends from church would be there. There would definitely be beer. He didn't really like beer all that much, but he would never tell his friends that. He had been drunk a couple of times, and he felt guilty because he knew it was wrong. He really didn't remember much about those experiences, although he did remember

the way he felt afterwards. "Not worth it" was the way he would sum it up. He wondered if Mitch the "medicine man" would show up with his stash of pills. Jaren figured the pills were basically harmless, but he didn't get why everyone acted like they were such a big deal. He knew they would be thinking how uncool he was if he didn't do them too, but he really didn't want to. He just wanted to go out and have a good time with his friends. He knew could do that without any help.

Jaren sighed as he got up and started to change clothes in anticipation of the night ahead of him. "Oh well," he thought. "Maybe next weekend I'll just go see the new Schwarzenegger flick."

What do you think Jaren is likely to do at the party? Why?
He will likely drink beer, which he doesn't even like, and take drugs, which he really doesn't want to do because he won't want his actions to be contrary to the actions of "everyone else."

How do you think he will justify his actions?
Possible answers: It won't really hurt me anyway. Everyone will think I'm uncool if I don't go along.

Do you think Jaren walks in integrity?
There is no way he lives a life of integrity if he is too weak to stand up for what is right in favor of going along with the crowd.

Jaren believes that if he goes against the others, they will reject him. What do you think might also happen if he begins to take a stand for what is right?
God honors obedience. We limit Him when we assume that our positive actions will have negative repercussions. Romans 12:9 says, "Do not be overcome by evil, but overcome evil with good." In standing up for what is right, Jaren would be overcoming evil with good, and the Lord could use that to impact the lives of many people.

25. Nehemiah did not see his position as governor as an excuse to demonstrate his power and exert his influence. Instead, he participated in the lowly labor of the masses by working on the wall with them. He saw his position as a means of serving. What does this tell us about integrity?
Integrity involves the selfless serving of others. It is not just doing what is right when no one is looking, but it is doing what is Christlike when no one would even expect it or ask for it.

26. How does Nehemiah demonstrate that integrity isn't proud or boastful?
He didn't encourage people to serve others while he had servants tending to him, which would be justified by his position. He demonstrated that integrity loves and serves.

DAY 4

 FOCUS

Joseph refused to give in to temptation with Potiphar's wife, but was unjustly accused and sent to prison. Because he obeyed God, the Lord caused Joseph to prosper and he eventually became Pharaoh's Prime Minister, saving many lives because of his position. Regardless of the difficulty of our circumstances, when we refuse to give in to temptation and choose to walk in integrity, God will honor our obedience.

 APPLICATION

32. What personal characteristics do you think Joseph displayed in his daily life that would have caused Potiphar to entrust so much to him?
Possible answers: honesty, trustworthiness, wisdom, sincerity, integrity, etc.

45. We never read about Joseph grumbling in jail about his troubles and how unfair it had all been. He couldn't see the big picture of what would happen in his life as a result of his imprisonment, and all the good he would ultimately do for so many people, including his own family. What must Joseph have realized while unjustly forced to sit in that cell?
God is bigger than any kind of tribulation that can come our way. Not only does He see the big picture, but He controls it, and He can cause good to come out of any circumstance, no matter how bad it may seem at the time.

47. Describe the chain of events you think would have occurred if, instead of resisting the temptation, Joseph had given in to it. Do you think anything would have been different if he had sinned with Potiphar's wife?
If Joseph had given in to temptation, he not only would have lost his position with Potiphar, but he could have lost his life over it. Even if Potiphar had spared Joseph's life, he would have lost everything, including his character and his reputation, because although sin promises joy, excitement, and content-

ment, sin does not keep its promises. Joseph knew that if He stayed focused on God and continued to walk in integrity, obeying His commands, God would take care of Him. And He did.

48. How is it possible to walk in integrity in the midst of a perverse world? How do you say "no" when even other Christians are willing to compromise in the gray areas?
You can't base your level of commitment on the assurance of someone else's commitment. And you can't resist the temptations that the world has to offer on your own. The only way to be a person of integrity is through abiding in Christ: seeking Him, learning of Him, and drawing from His life.

DAY 5

 FOCUS

Daniel refused to refrain from praying to God and to pray to King Darius instead and was thrown into the lion's den as a result. Yet God closed the mouths of the lions, miraculously saving him. Because of Daniel's integrity, God was glorified, just as the result of our integrity is that God is glorified as well. When we trust Him and obey His commands, He will work our obedience for a greater glory.

 APPLICATION

50. Verse 3 tells us that Daniel possessed an "extraordinary spirit" (NAS). What characteristics do you think made up such a spirit?
Possible answers: optimism, compassion, encouragement, the ability to be content in varying circumstances, etc.

52. Why do you think the king's advisers proposed a law that banned praying to any god and only permitted praying to King Darius?
They knew Daniel already prayed to God three times a day. And knowing Daniel's integrity, they obviously knew that he would not be willing to compromise in this area.

58. After completing this study, what do you think integrity accomplishes, and what will be the result if we walk in it daily?
Integrity glorifies God. If we trust in Him and walk in integrity, He will work our obedience for great things.

WEEK 25
FAITHFULNESS

DISCUSSION

When you think about faithfulness, what comes to mind?
Possible answers: a person who is full of faith, trusting, or a person who is true to his word.

We tend to focus on our own faithfulness in our relationship with God. Do we trust Him? Are we loyal to Him, His laws, and His service? Thinking of your own experience, how has God been faithful to you?

DAY 1

FOCUS

Many aspects make up faithfulness, including truthfulness, trustworthiness, action, and dependability. Our faithfulness in all areas is based on God's faithfulness to us. Although we sin, He does not break His covenant with His people. He started a good work in us when we accepted Him, and He is faithful to complete that work in us as we grow in Him.

APPLICATION

7. According to Philippians 1:6, God is faithful to finish what He started in us as believers. What means has He already provided for you that will enable you to grow in your Christian walk?
Possible answers: discipleship classes and studies, the Bible, discipleship team leaders, your church.

This year, we have been learning about the characteristics God wants us to demonstrate in our everyday lives. How does His faithfulness relate to these characteristics?
God enables us to live out those characteristics daily, even regardless of our circumstances. Without the power of His Holy Spirit in our lives, we would not have the ability to do it.

According to 1 Thessalonians 5:24, He is faithful to His call in our lives. If we have been called into the ministry, for example, He is faithful to work that call to completion, opening the doors that will enable it to happen. **What is His call for all believers, which He also is faithful to finish in us?**
His call to believers is that we be witnesses for Him.

First John 1:9 says He is faithful to forgive us of our sins. **Is His faithfulness to do so based on our ability to confess them? Is it based on the faithfulness of those who pray for us?**
Although we are instructed to confess our sins, His faithfulness to forgive us is not based on any ability or action of our own. Instead, it is based on Christ, who made forgiveness of sin possible.

11. What should His faithfulness produce in us?
It produces in us the motive to be faithful. His faithfulness to us makes our faithfulness possible.

2 Thessalonians 3:3
When the evil one throws temptation in our path, on what can we base our ability to resist it?
We can base it on God's faithfulness to enable us to resist it, and not on any source of courage or strength we may attempt to work up within ourselves.

DAY 2

FOCUS

Jesus told the parable of the good slave, who was faithful in accomplishing a small task even when the master was away, and an evil slave who proved himself to be unfaithful because, in convincing himself that the master would not be returning for a long time, he neglected his duty. In the same way, the Lord has removed His physical presence from us in order to see if we will be faithful to Him.

⚒ APPLICATION

13. Would you consider this responsibility to be great or relatively small and simple?
It is a single, relatively easy task.

15. The slave was faithful and sensible because of his good action. How does this fact apply to our lives, based on James 1:22, which says, "But prove yourselves doers of the word, and not merely hearers who delude themselves"?
Faithfulness isn't just memorizing verses and having great spiritual knowledge. Instead, it is living out our faith in our everyday actions.

17. Since the slave thought his master would not be coming back for a long time, how did he view his responsibilities?
He viewed them as insignificant. He convinced himself that he had no real responsibilities. He saw his work as something that he could put off until later.

19. It is interesting that the evil slave didn't just neglect his duties, but he actually went to the other extreme. He chose to follow a path of sin. We are guilty of the same when we refuse to make a commitment to follow Christ. Making no commitment at all is making a commitment to sin. How do we attempt to justify such a decision?
We convince ourselves that the Master isn't coming back for a very long time. We decide to follow Him, but only on our own terms: going just so far and then no farther, especially when it involves self sacrifice.

21. "If God wants us to believe in Him, why doesn't He just show Himself to us?"
"If God wants people to know He exists, why doesn't He work some kind of miracle to prove Himself?"

Unbelievers may ask such questions in order to justify their unbelief. Just as the master in this parable learned who could be trusted by removing his physical presence from them, how does God do the same?
He removes His presence in order to see who will be faithful to Him. As He said to Thomas, "Blessed are they who did not see, and yet believed." John 20:29b

In reality, how did God show Himself to us?
God showed Himself to us in the form of His Son.

23. If you knew that Jesus was coming back this week, what would you do and what would you change in order to make yourself ready for His coming?

BARCLAY QUOTATION
Is the sense of God's presence different in the halls of your high school than it is in the pews of your church? What does our response in these different environments show the Master?
Although the sense of His presence may be different, He is there, in the halls at school, watching. And He is looking to see who will be faithful to Him, even when His presence isn't noticed.

27. The good slave was given the task of feeding the members of the household at the proper time, and in this he proved faithful. As believers, we can relate to this task. How are we charged with the responsibility of feeding others at the proper time?
We are given the responsibility of sharing Christ with others.

In this, have you shown yourself to be faithful or unfaithful?

DAY 3

FOCUS
Jesus told a parable in Luke 16 using an unrighteous person to teach us about righteousness. Although we may not put forth a great amount of fervor in doing wrong, we must examine ourselves in terms of our fervor in doing right. If we put forth the same amount of effort in our Christian walk as we do in secular areas of our lives, great things could be accomplished for the Lord's kingdom.

⚒ APPLICATION
32. What do you think the world would be like if Christians gave 100 percent in living out their faith?
Christians would be what their name implies: they would be like Christ. They would know God intimately and far greater numbers of people would be won to Him because of it.

33. Sometimes it takes a great deal of foresight to see the potential in others. If we, as Christians, were able to look beyond the sin of the guy who uses vulgar language in nearly every sentence and the girl who has "been with" nearly every guy in the senior class, what would be the result?
If we could see beyond the sin to what they could become in Christ, we would be more likely to devote our lives to discipling them.

35. Is your biggest goal to achieve the American dream: to work hard, make money, retire, and live the good life?

Do you spend more time thinking about the luxuries you would like to have than you do thinking about the needs of others? Do you find yourself throwing away small amounts of money on another knickknack to put on your dresser, another afternoon playing video games, or another pair of shoes to wear? Where, instead, should your money be directed?

It should be directed toward things that are eternal: securing friends in heaven.

DAY 4

 ## FOCUS

According to Luke 16:10, a person who has been faithful in a very small task can be trusted to be faithful in a large one. Although we might be tempted to consider the small things to be unworthy of our efforts, they are the testing ground for our commitment to overall faithfulness. If we want the Lord to reveal His will to us in regard to the future, we must be faithful with what He has already revealed to us to be His will, such as walking in integrity and obedience in all areas.

APPLICATION

 ## LIFE SITUATION

38. "Oh, yeah, that's right, we do have play practice tonight," Erma sounded disappointed. "Well, I guess that means we can't catch that big sale at the mall."

"Yeah," said Julianne. "And I really need to get my prom dress. I mean, it's not like there's much time left or anything."

"And I know for a fact the sale ends today. Why did Ms. Velasquez call an extra practice anyway? There are still two weeks before the play," Erma whined.

"Yeah, but she'll be hacked if we don't show."

"Why would she? I mean, it's not like our parts are important or anything. We are just in the choir. We wouldn't even be missed," Erma rationalized.

"True," her friend agreed. "You know, if we had really important parts like Hassan or Joanna, it would be different. But since we don't, I think we should just skip out."

"I was hoping you would see things my way," Erma smiled as she grabbed her car keys. "Let's hit the mall!"

Julianne and Erma came up with many reasons for not going to play practice. They didn't have an important role. They probably wouldn't be missed. Their teacher shouldn't have scheduled the practice and messed up their plans in the first place. What was the real reason they skipped play practice?

They decided to go to the mall because it was more important than following through on a commitment.

Do you think if the girls had a major role in the play, like Hassan or Joanna, they would have given up the shopping opportunity to attend the play practice?

The girls probably would have found other reasons to justify their absence, even if they did have major roles in the play. People are more likely to be faithful to something for which they will receive recognition. If our name is in the program, we will look bad if the play is unsuccessful. In the small things, such as attending a practice when your role seems insignificant, there is little applause from the crowd.

When there is no applause from the crowd, why should we still strive to be faithful?

When others don't see, recognize, or appreciate our efforts, the Lord does. And we must always reflect on whether we are attempting to glorify ourselves or if our intention is to glorify God.

Do you think Ms. Velasquez will give the girls a leading role in the next program?

Because they weren't faithful to show up to practice when they were members of the choir, she will likely decide that she can't trust them in a leading role.

39. How are we likely to respond to the Holy Spirit's conviction when we aren't faithful in a little thing?

If we view the little things as insignificant, then we will likely get over them more easily than we would if we were being convicted for our lack of faith in something we see as important. We might not give them the consideration they deserve because it is easy to just move on.

40. Explain the following sentence: "If I want God to reveal His will to me regarding the future, then I will be faithful to accomplish today what He has already revealed to me to be His will."

Possible answers: We know that it is God's will that we seek Him. If we are faithful in doing so, He will not only be more likely to reveal His will to us regarding the future.

43. A person who is not faithful in service will not only be unfaithful in a position of leadership, but he or she will likely never be given the position in the first place. How will this fact become evident when, for example, you begin your career?

You have to start at the bottom to get to the top. In a large corporation, even those with college degrees often start out in the mail room. Those with the "I'm too good for this job" attitude or who fail to do a good job because they think their work is unimportant will be overlooked for promotions. However, those who are committed to work hard even when performing lowly tasks will likely be the first ones placed in positions of leadership.

DAY 5

FOCUS

David and Jonathan give us an excellent example of faithfulness in friendship. Because their relationship with the Lord served as the bond between them, David could trust Jonathan to be truthful with him regarding his father Saul's plot to kill him. It is only through basing our friendships on God rather than on the qualities we admire in our friends themselves that our relationships will be faithful.

APPLICATION

48. Jonathan demonstrated his faithfulness as a friend to David. According to Luke 16:10, what are some examples of ways we can show ourselves to be faithful friends to others?

Possible answers: According to this verse, we are faithful to our friends in the very little things that make up our relationships with them. We can be faithful by not betraying a confidence, by listening to them when they are going through difficulties, by not gossiping about them, by doing them favors and expecting nothing in return.

50. Imagine that your father is the king, and all of your life you have been promised the throne. Then, the Lord begins to reveal to you that this is not His plan. Instead, it will be your best friend who will become the future king. How does Jonathan's attitude toward David in this situation demonstrate his own faithfulness to God?

He knew it was God's plan for David to be king and he also knew that God's plan was better than his own or his father's. Jonathan's faithfulness to God is demonstrated in his desire to submit to God's will,

even though it meant forfeiting a kingdom.

53. Pick the best phrase to complete the sentence. The relationship between David and Jonathan was strong because...

...they both came from the same socioeconomic background.
...they had many things in common.
...they had spent so much of their "growing up" years together.
...their families were close.
...they were better than everyone else.

None of the phrases makes the sentence true. David and Jonathan had a strong friendship because the Lord was their bond.

57. Why would Jonathan have had the right to be grieved for himself?

He was about to lose his future kingdom. His father had just uttered profanities at him and had even thrown a spear at him to strike him down in his anger. Jonathan could have been deeply hurt by the way his father treated him, yet he was not grieved for himself.

60. Because the Lord was their bond, David and Jonathan could see the nature of God reflected in each other. This was the key to the strength of their relationship. If, during the course of their friendship, for example, Jonathan had heard rumors that David was saying things about him behind his back, how do you think Jonathan would have responded?

He would have known the rumors were untrue because he could have trusted David completely, just as he would have trusted God.

Sometimes our faithful friends need to tell us what is true, even if what they have to say is something we don't want to hear. If you have a friendship with someone in which the Lord is your bond, how would you respond if your friend told you that the person you were dating had become, for example, involved in selling drugs?

You would know you could trust him or her because his or her motives would be pure. Your friend would be looking out for your best interests out of love, so you wouldn't have to wonder if he or she just wanted to break up your relationship so that he or she could date the person you were seeing.

WEEK 26
GENTLENESS

DAY 1

 ### FOCUS

The only words Jesus ever used to describe Himself were humble and gentle. Because He placed such emphasis on living out these attributes, so must we pursue them in our lives as we abide in Him.

 ### APPLICATION

3. Why do you think Jesus only used words in this single instance to describe Himself?
Jesus was more intent on how He lived His life than He was interested in describing Himself.

Why does this give us an added reason to pursue gentleness in our own lifestyles?
We know Jesus was humble and gentle not only by the way He lived, but also because He put such emphasis on these characteristics that He used them to describe Himself. If we are to pursue Christlikeness, we must pursue these attributes.

4. In what ways, rather than in pursuing Christ, do non-Christians attempt to find rest for their souls?
Possible answers: relationships, therapy, alcohol.

In what ways, other than in pursuing Christ, do Christians attempt to find rest for their souls?
Possible answers: relationships, church work, recreational activities, counseling.

Do you think people can ever truly find rest for their souls outside of an intimate relationship with Christ?
No. Salvation is the prerequisite and an ongoing, learning relationship with Him is the only way to experience rest. John 15:5 says, "I am the vine, you are the branches; he who abides in Me, and I in him, he bears much fruit; for apart from Me you can do nothing."

6. Why do you think Christians are unwilling to take His yoke, considering the fact that His yoke is easy and His load is light?
Possible answers: They want to maintain control. They mistakenly see His yoke as being heavy and burdensome. He is not their top priority.

7. Think of someone you know who has a gentle spirit. What draws you to such a person?
Possible answers: kindness, patience, she makes you feel at ease, he doesn't force his opinions on you.

How can you learn from him or her?
You can learn from this person by observing his or her life. Learn from his or her words, attitudes, responses to pressure, commitment to Christ, and interaction with friends, acquaintances, and strangers.

DAY 2

 ### FOCUS

Humility and meekness are indications of gentleness and were demonstrated in the life of Christ. Gentleness describes how we should treat others, while meekness describes how we should respond when mistreated by others. Gentleness is humility in action because it is submitting to the Lord's control and the committing to obey Him.

 ### APPLICATION

9. What does the world believe to be the preferred circumstances concerning. . .
...a person's birth?
Possible answers: noble birth, being born to a wealthy family, or having famous parents.
...submission?
Possible answers: standing up for your rights, not giving in, not submitting to others because shows weakness, or it is better to be the one in control.

...occupation?

Possible answers: it should be prestigious, highly respected, it should be high-paying, or it should require great skill and intelligence to perform.

...possessions?

Possible answers: obtain as many material possessions as possible, they will make you happy, buy the more expensive brands because they will make you look better, or sell things you no longer want (instead of giving them away) so you'll make some money and can buy more things.

...death?

Possible answers: be mourned and remembered by many, die peacefully of old age, or have many people at your funeral.

What does the fact that Jesus defied all of these preferred circumstances tell you about their value?

What the world says is ideal or preferred is not necessarily what is preferred by God. In fact, this is rarely the case.

BRIDGES QUOTATION

Indicate which of the following words would be associated with gentleness and which would be associated with meekness. Some are associated with both.

a. considerate
b. kind
c. submissive
d. patient
e. gracious
f. humble
g. calm
h. softhearted
i. mild
j. tender
k. peacemaker
l. turning the other cheek

(Gentleness: a; e; h; i; j;   Meekness: c; k; l;
Gentleness and meekness: b; d; f; g)

13. How are all characteristics of Christlikeness really humility in action?

They are all a result of humbling ourselves in submission to God's will and in obedience to Him.

SWINDOLL QUOTATION

 LIFE SITUATION

Instructions: Review the characteristics of gentleness mentioned in the Charles Swindoll quotation: having strength under control, being calm and peaceful when surrounded by a heated atmosphere, emitting a soothing effect on those who may be angry or otherwise beside themselves, possessing tact and gracious courtesy that causes others to retain their self esteem and dignity, and Christlikeness.

Then read through the following conversation among some friends in the hall at school. You will be a participant named Adrienne. When it is indicated that Adrienne speaks or acts, apply the principles of gentleness in his or her attitude, actions, or words. Adrienne's first response is given.

Note: This could also be conducted as a role-playing situation by assigning parts to various students.

"You can't be serious!" Georgette exclaimed. "He actually stood you up?"

"I couldn't believe it," Allie shook her head. "I mean, I am so humiliated!"

"That doesn't really sound like Ryan to me," Adrienne said. "You know, he's really _____."

"It may not be what you'd think he would do, but he sure did it to me," Allie struggled to hold back the tears.

Adrienne _____ (action, then words).

"Well, all I know is that now I feel completely worthless. I mean, being stood up! Ryan is cruel and I hate him for doing this to me!" Allie's hurt feelings were being replaced by anger.

"Oh my gosh, here he comes now!" exclaimed Miranda.

"Well I'm not gonna stick around to hear his excuses. He's already embarrassed me enough!" Allie quickly made her way to the restroom.

"Hey guys, what's going on?" Ryan asked as he joined the group.

"You know what's going on!" There was anger in Georgette's eyes. "You've got some nerve!"

Adrienne said, "_____."

"Allie told us all about Friday night," Georgette stated. "So, just exactly where were you, huh?"

"What do you mean, where was I? I was at my grandparents' for our family reunion. What's it to ya, anyway?"

Adrienne said, "_____."

"Oh, I get it. She thought our date was last weekend, I guess. But we weren't supposed to go out last Friday. I asked Allie out for next Friday." He said.

"Well she sure didn't know that!" Miranda was obviously angry too. "And I'm not so sure you didn't just plan this to hurt her anyway. You do have a reputation for being a jerk sometimes, you know!"

"_____" Adrienne said to Miranda.

"_____," Adrienne told Ryan.

"Yeah," Georgette chimed in. "You better do some pretty quick apologizing!"

"O. K. gang, let's get to class now!" The vice principal said as he approached the group.

As the students went their separate ways, Adrienne and Georgette walked toward their fourth-hour class. "_____," Adrienne said to Georgette.

Possible answers: "not the kind of guy who would do something like that on purpose. Maybe there's a good reason."
put his/her arm around Allie. "Why don't you just talk to him about it?"
"Hi, Ryan. We're just getting ready to go to class."
"Well, I think you probably should talk to Allie. She's really upset, but maybe it's all a misunderstanding."
"I don't think he did it on purpose." "I'm sure if you talk to her everything will be all right."
"I'm sorry Allie got her feelings hurt, too. But I'm sure Ryan will do the right thing."

What are the obvious benefits of applying the principles of gentleness to any situation?
Possible answers: Gentleness in situations where there is conflict likely lends itself to peacemaking. Gentleness in times of anger will likely have a calming effect. Gentle attitudes, actions, and words may encourage the same gentle spirit from others.

DAY 3

 FOCUS
In spite of the law and the Pharisees, Jesus healed a man of his withered hand on the Sabbath because of the man's value to Him. We must treat a Christian who has fallen into sin gently, just as Christ is gentle and patient with us in the midst of our own sin.

 APPLICATION
18. Jesus did not argue the points of the law with the Pharisees, although He certainly could have done so. Why, instead, did He choose to spend His time healing the people?
It was more important to do good than it was to win an argument, even though He was clearly right. Jesus saw the people needing healing as much more valuable and worthy of His time than putting the Pharisees in their place.

19. Many people equate gentleness with staying out of problems so as not to stir up trouble. Jesus didn't quit healing the people in order to avoid the wrath of the Pharisees. Instead, He withdrew from the troublemakers. What can we learn from this?
We should seek to do good where it is needed and

not subject ourselves to those who may ridicule us in the process. Continuing to do what is right in the face of opposition is one aspect of gentleness in action.

Although Jesus could have been tempted to confront the Pharisees, whose plan was He sensitive to and most concerned with?
He was concerned about God's plan and living in obedience to Him.

24. Why might you be more likely to treat some relationships more gently than others?
The more you value the relationship, the more cautious and gentle you will be in handling it.

If you choose to break a fragile crystal glass, you have obviously destroyed it. But how can the destruction be even more widespread than just ruining a single crystal glass? How does this relate to destroying a fragile Christian?
Broken glass is a hazard to all who come into contact with it. In the same way, if we destroy a fragile Christian through destructive words and actions, his or her impact on others could be harmful as well.

25. What kind of person would you characterize as a smoldering wick or a battered reed?
It is a Christian who is greatly weakened through adverse circumstances, oppression from the enemy, or embracing unconfessed sin.

Why do you think Jesus never gives up on such a person?
Jesus sees the potential of what a person can become if he or she knows Him.

Why must we treat all people with gentleness in terms of their sin, even if they do not appear to be a smoldering wick or a battered reed?
What a person appears to be on the outside may not be compatible with what he or she is experiencing on the inside.

31. What does a harsh approach and condemning attitude do for a smoldering wick?
It puts the smoldering wick out.

 ACTIVITY
Instructions: Bring to the discipleship session objects that we treat gently, such as a sandwich, a drinking glass and two flowers. Cut the sandwich in half and then crush one of the halves. Tear up one flower.

What is the result when something is not treated gently?
It is destroyed. It is a smoldering wick that goes out and a battered reed that breaks off.

We all have the power to break a glass, crush a sandwich, and tear up a flower. We apply gentleness to objects and people in one form or another every day, even though we have the power to destroy. Why do we hold back?
The reason we are gentle with objects and relationships is because they have value to us.

DAY 4

 FOCUS

Although the Lord possesses all strength and control, He approaches us with a spirit of gentleness. In establishing the church at Thessalonica, Paul, too, approached the people in a gentle manner rather than authoritatively or with impure motives. When we approach all of our relationships with a gentle spirit, people will see Christ in us and are likely to respond to us in the same way.

 APPLICATION

37. When a person has a great deal of knowledge in a certain area, as well as a great deal of authority to make decisions concerning it as Paul did in establishing the church at Thessalonica, how might he or she tend to respond to those under his or her authority?
Possible answers: with a certain amount of pride, a condescending attitude, authoritative, or harsh.

What type of response might this person receive from those under his or her authority?
Possible answers:resentment, rebellion, or anger.

What type of response might a person with a great deal of knowledge and authority receive from those under his authority when he treats them with gentleness instead?
Possible answers: loyalty, appreciation, love, cooperation.

 LIFE SITUATION

Yolanda and Estelle have never been friends. Yolanda doesn't like the way Estelle uses people. Estelle doesn't like the way Yolanda talks badly about others behind their backs, including her best friends. Estelle looks at Yolanda with hatred whenever their eyes meet. Yolanda acts as though she is superior to Estelle. On the rare occasions when they speak to each other, it is usually to say something along the lines of, "Do you think you could manage to get out of my way so I can get by?" or "Yeah, like you could get someone to go out with you!" It has been this way between the two of them for as long as either of them can remember.

Why do you think Yolanda and Estelle continue to dislike each other?
Most likely, they continue to dislike each other because of pride. Bad attitudes, rude comments, and evil thoughts continue in a vicious cycle and grow when fed upon. Yolanda is unkind to Estelle because Estelle is unkind to Yolanda. They have never had any reason to act otherwise.

What do you think might happen if, when Yolanda gave Estelle a dirty look, Estelle looked at Yolanda with kindness in her eyes? Or if, when Estelle made a rude comment about something Yolanda was wearing, Yolanda complimented Estelle's outfit?
It is possible that over time, a new kind of relationship could develop. If one of the girls began approaching the other with a gentle spirit, it might open the door for the Lord to do something in the heart of the other.

DAY 5

 FOCUS

Gentleness is manifested in each of us through our tongues, eyes, hands, and personalities, and any relationship benefits from it. We should pursue gentleness because it is precious in the sight of God.

 APPLICATION

45. In Galatians 5:22-23 where Paul describes the fruit of the Spirit, gentleness and self-control are mentioned together. How do you think the two relate to each other?
It takes great self-control to approach all people and situations in a spirit of gentleness.

48. Briefly list the characteristics that describe the average friendship and the friendship that is characterized by a gentle spirit.

WEEK 27
MERCY AND FORGIVENESS

DAY 1

FOCUS

Because God, in Christ, has graciously forgiven us of our sins, we must forgive others as we pursue Christlikeness. If we are unable to forgive others, we are blind to our own need for forgiveness. When forgiving someone is contrary to our emotions, it becomes an act of the will to choose to obey God.

APPLICATION

3. Paul tells the believers who they are before he tells them what to do. How could Colossians 3:12 be restated in order to bring the two aspects together?
"Because you are holy, act holy; Because you are chosen, act chosen; Because you are beloved, act beloved."

8. You are angry with a person who has wronged you, and the hurt, as well as the rift in your relationship, has gone on for some time. Finally, you decide that your friendship is more important than your hurt feelings so you decide to forget about it so you can go back to being friends again. Because you are able to put the past behind you, does this signal that you have forgiven the person?
Forgiveness is not synonymous with forgetting. In fact, you can forget about a wrong without ever forgiving it. The problem lies in the fact that memories of the incident will bring up the hurt again when forgiveness has not taken place.

How can you possibly tear up the IOU when you would rather wave it in the person's face and demand payment?
Tearing up the IOU is an act of the will. It is making a choice to obey God, and leaving it to Him to bring about the feelings of forgiveness in His time.

DAY 2

FOCUS

Jesus told the parable of the slave who was forgiven a great debt by the king but was unwilling himself to forgive the lesser debt of his fellow slave. Because the Lord has graciously canceled out the great debt we owe on account of our sin, we must likewise forgive others of their sins against us without exception. When we fail to forgive others, it is a demonstration that we do not truly understand the depth of God's compassion and forgiveness in our own lives.

APPLICATION

11. What does the Lord have the right to do with us on account of our sin?
He has the right to take everything from us including our own lives. He has the right to cast us into hell.

12. Why do you think the slave promised to repay the king when it was obvious that no one could repay such a huge debt?
He may have just been buying time, or he may have not had a true understanding of just how indebted he was to the king. Those who think they can repay God for their debt of sin do not have a clear understanding of their level of indebtedness. It isn't possible to repay a debt that has been wiped out by forgiveness.

13. As in verse 27, why do you think the Lord is willing to cancel out our debt?
He has compassion on us.

If someone owed us a great deal of money, what might we do that in today's terms would seem to be a demonstration of mercy toward him or her?
Humanly speaking, we could extend the note, without interest if we are truly compassionate. We could reduce the amount owed to us. However, divine mercy and forgiveness would tear up the note.

14. How do we act in the same way as this slave in our own relationships with others?

We might say "if I have to pay, so does he." Or we might say "if she doesn't forgive me, I won't forgive her." If we feel that we owe God for our sin, then we will feel that others owe us for their sins against us. This is a result of not understanding who we are in Christ. "He made Him who knew no sin to be sin on our behalf, that we might become the righteousness of God in Him." (2 Corinthians 5:21)

15. A denarius was the same as one day's wage. To what might we compare the magnitude of the debt the second slave owed the first in terms of our relationships with others today? Use your imagination.

The second slave owed the first a great deal of money. If a person worked all day and earned $50, this slave owed the other $5,000. It could be compared, for example, to a person who carelessly and recklessly totaled her best friend's car and then refused to pay for it.

Because this slave owed so much (compare it to $5,000), did he have the right to demand payment from the second slave? Can a person be expected to forgive someone who carelessly wrecked her car?

The first slave was not justified in his response to the second slave in comparison to his own debt that was graciously canceled out. And the person who fails to forgive someone, regardless of the reason, is not justified when compared to his or her own debt which the Lord has canceled out.

21. What do you think Peter was thinking when he asked Jesus if he should forgive his brother seven times?

He was probably thinking that his view of forgiveness was very merciful. After all, he wasn't just giving his brother a second chance, he was giving him seven.

If you are keeping track of the number of times you have forgiven a person, what does that say about the quality of the forgiveness you have shown him or her?

If you are keeping score, then you haven't really forgiven him or her from your heart. In fact, because you are keeping track of the wrongs, you may even be reserving them and protecting the memories of them so you can throw them back at the person at another time.

DAY 3

 FOCUS

When a person has wronged us, we experience forgiveness through our willingness to forgive the offender. When we have wronged another, we experience forgiveness through our willingness to repent and seek forgiveness. A sinner can only receive Christ's forgiveness through repentance.

APPLICATION

LIFE SITUATION

Kelsie walked across the parking lot, heading toward her car, when she glanced over at the tennis court to see if her friend Victor was still lobbing tennis balls after practice. She caught sight of Dionne, rushing to her own car as if she were in a hurry. "Hi, Dionne!" Kelsie shouted. Dionne looked her way, but did not respond. Instead, she got in her car and quickly drove away.

"Well, what is her problem?" Kelsie thought. "She just completely blew me off! Why in the world would she act that way?"

Kelsie tried to think back to see if she could determine what might be the problem. "She's probably mad at me because my SAT score was higher than hers. Or maybe it's because Patrice asked me to go to the concert with her instead of asking Dionne. What a baby! It's not like she and Patrice are joined at the hip or anything, just because she calls her her best friend. I bet she thinks I'm trying to be buddy-buddy with Patrice. She probably thinks I told Patrice not to ask her to go to that concert. Who knows? She's probably talking bad about me to everyone she sees. She sure has a way of doing thât!" Kelsie's anger and resentment began to grow.

"Hey, are you ready to go?" Asked Maleek as she approached Kelsie.

"What? Oh. . .yeah, I'm ready."

"What's going on? You look like you're a million miles away!"

"I was just thinking about Dionne."

"Yeah? What's she up to?" asked Maleek.

"Being a snob!" Kelsie responded.

"What?"

"Well, I just said 'Hi' to her and she just, you know, looked right through me. She didn't say a word. She just drove off like a maniac or something. She's probably mad at me. I just can't stand people like that!"

"Gosh, I wonder what her problem is," Maleek said.

"But you know...come to think of it, Dionne was acting kind of snobbish to me earlier this week. I can't remember what the deal was, but I do remember she was acting like she didn't want to give me the time of day."

"Well I think I should just give her a taste of her own medicine! I don't care if we are lab partners. She'll just have to work on that chemistry project by herself. I know! I'll just tell Mr. McReynolds that I just can't work with her. He'll have to assign me to somebody else!"

"Yeah! That'll show her!" Maleek agreed. "Maybe she'll get reassigned to Norbert Hollinger!"

"Yeah!" Kelsie laughed. "That would sure serve her right!" The two girls continued to laugh as they got into Kelsie's car and drove off.

How did Kelsie let her imagination run away with her in this situation?

She interpreted Dionne's failure to respond to her as an insult directed toward her. She came up with a reason why Dionne did not talk to her and instead of treating it as a theory, she treated it as fact and responded negatively as a result.

What do you think is now Maleek's attitude toward Dionne?

Maleek is mad at Dionne as well because she snubbed her friend Kelsie and because she now thinks she remembers being snubbed by Dionne last week.

What action do you think the girls will now take?

They will not only probably refuse to talk to Dionne, but chances are they will talk to others about Dionne.

If Kelsie had used self-control when it came to her thought life, she could have reached a different conclusion about Dionne and avoided a problem that had the potential to grow into a disaster. What is an example of a thought sequence that would have produced a more positive result?

Possible answers: "I wonder what's wrong with Dionne? I hope I haven't done anything to make her mad or hurt her feelings. She may have not even heard me when I said 'Hi.' Or she may have had something else on her mind. I've done that before when I've been thinking about something. I'll just call her later tonight and make sure everything's OK."

Instead of talking to Maleek about the problem, what should Kelsie have done?

She should have talked to Dionne not Maleek. She should have approached her in a non-threatening, pleasant manner the next time she saw her. She could have mentioned that she saw her in the parking lot, or she could have not mentioned the incident to Dionne at all. She should have run from the temptation to gossip.

Let's say the girls were right about Dionne, that she was trying to snub them. How could they avoid sinning even if they were right?

They could decide not to be angry with her and not hold a grudge against her. They could be friendly to her in spite of her attitude. They could treat her with respect even though she did not return the favor. They could conduct themselves in such a manner that she would not have any reason to criticize them to others. (1 Peter 3:16)

29. Is it harder to say "I'm sorry," or is it harder to say, "Will you forgive me?" Explain.

A person can say, "I'm sorry," without really feeling sorry. Apologizing in this way also keeps the focus on the offender. However, when a person says, "Will you forgive me?" it is a result of a humble attitude and it shifts the focus to the offended person. It is often a reflection of a more heartfelt, repentant attitude.

What is your responsibility when you repent but the person refuses to forgive you?

In this situation, you have taken care of your part of forgiveness. The person may not forgive you, but the Lord does. And He tells us that "If possible, so far as it depends on you, be at peace with all men." (Romans 12:18)

What lives and grows in the heart of a person who refuses to forgive?

Possible answers: bitterness, loneliness, anger, hatred, resentment, or misery.

DAY 4

 **FOCUS**

Although Saul gathered 3,000 men for the purpose of taking David's life, David showed Saul great mercy when he had the opportunity to kill him but instead spared his life. David left the discipline of Saul's sin in the hand of the Lord. We should see chance meetings with our enemies as opportunities to show them mercy in both words and actions. Mercy in forgiveness is only possible when it is not deserved.

 **APPLICATION**

45. When a person is shown great mercy, how is he or she likely to respond to the one who showed it?
He or she is likely to respond with great appreciation, joy, and in many cases, wonder. When a person realizes that he or she has been shown great mercy, it is often an avenue that leads to repentance.

47. How has God demonstrated His abundant mercy in your life?
He saved us when we clearly did not deserve it. (Matthew 9:13, Titus 3:5)

DAY 5

 **FOCUS**

A person who is judgmental is unable to show mercy. Jesus instructs us to remove the "log" from our own eye before attempting to remove the "speck" from someone else's. Only a person who is truly humble, meek, and pure can see clearly to bring specific sins in a person's life to his or her attention.

APPLICATION

51. If you have a log in your own eye, yet in spite of the way it obstructs your view, you are still able to detect a speck in someone else's eye, what must be true about you?
You are trying to find a fault in someone else.

54. What do you think will happen if there is no one to call to your attention specific sins in your life or if you are not receptive to what the person has to say?
You are likely to discover that the sin will grow. When we continue in our sin, we may find that our consciences become calloused. Everyone else may see it, but because we have given in to it for so long, we don't.

When you get something in your eye, it causes you a great deal of pain. Who would you ask to try and remove it for you: your five-year-old cousin, a friend across the street, or a registered nurse? Why?
You would be better off to have a nurse remove the object. The chances are greater that it will be removed as painlessly as possible.

How does this relate to having the right person bring to your attention a specific sin in your life?
It should be someone who is humble and nonjudg-

mental, someone you trust. If the "wrong" person calls to your attention a specific sin, it could cause more damage, just as a five-year-old would likely damage your eye in the process of trying to remove an object from it.

55. When someone has an object in his eye, why do we want to remove it for him?
Our desire to remove it should be a result of our concern for the person. We see that he is in pain and is greatly troubled because of it, so out of compassion, we want to help the person.

How ridiculous would it be to condemn a person for having a speck of dust in his or her eye?

ELLIOT QUOTATION
What will a person who is humble, childlike, pure, and meek be looking for when calling a specific sin to a person's attention?
He or she will be looking out for the interests and well-being of the person and not for any personal satisfaction. (Philippians 2:3-4)

WEEK 28
WISDOM

DAY 1

FOCUS

The real evidence of wisdom lies in a person's actions because actions are a reflection of the heart. Only the wisdom that comes from above is purely motivated. God, who is omniscient, will destroy the wisdom of this world because it is not of Him.

APPLICATION

1. We usually acknowledge the wisdom of old age because experience is the best teacher. What kind of experience do you think would be the best source of wisdom?

Experiencing God is the best means of obtaining wisdom because He is the source of it.

SANDERS QUOTATION

How does this quotation relate to James 1:22, "But prove yourselves doers of the Word, and not merely hearers who delude themselves"?

Hearers of the Word gain knowledge, but only those who are able to apply it through their words and deeds have the wisdom that comes from above.

Jeremiah 4:22

"For My people are foolish, They know Me not..." Why is it possible to be one of God's people and still not have wisdom when it comes to spiritual matters?

This verse clearly states that the source of foolishness is not knowing God. We can accept Christ without growing in our relationship with Him. Unfortunately, this is the case with many Christians. But we cannot hope to have the wisdom God readily gives if we do not devote ourselves to knowing Him.

8. At first it may seem excessive to think that the world is going to see the wisdom that comes from above as being from the devil. Yet the Pharisees openly claimed that Jesus received His power from Satan. When unbelievers see a person who is filled with the Spirit of the Lord, what are they likely to say or think about him or her?

Possible answers: the person is a Jesus freak, strange, a lunatic, or not in touch with the real world.

9. Unbelievers rarely acknowledge the wisdom of God. Whenever they attempt to refute Christian principles, they are saying that their wisdom exceeds God's wisdom. This seems foolish to us, yet how are we sometimes guilty of the same thing?

Possible answers: We are guilty of questioning the wisdom of God when we question things that happen in our lives: "Why did You allow this to happen?" or "Why me?" We doubt His wisdom when we think that we are somehow able to hide our sins from Him. We doubt His wisdom when we take a stance on ethical issues that is neither godly nor worldly but rather somewhere in the middle.

DAY 2

FOCUS

Solomon sought the God of his father David to be the Lord of his life as well. God was pleased with Solomon's request for wisdom in ruling His people and blessed Solomon with wisdom, riches, and fame. The Lord rewards those who are humble in acknowledging that they can do nothing apart from Him and who seek after the things He wants for them as well.

APPLICATION

11. What do you think would have happened if David, a man after God's own heart, had not passed on the value of this relationship to his son Solomon?

It undoubtedly would have changed the course of history. Solomon would not have been given wisdom from the Lord, and the prosperity Israel enjoyed as a result of Solomon's request would never have come to pass.

What does this say to us in terms of our own relationship with Christ as His disciples?
He must not only become our conviction, but we must pass on that conviction to others, ensuring that the next generation will follow Christ as well.

12. Solomon had been born to nobility and raised in prosperity. You would think that someone such as this would approach his position in life and new responsibilities with pride and even arrogance. Do you think his request was merely a result of false humility?
Solomon's humility was real. Otherwise God, who knows our hearts, would not have been pleased.

Solomon was confronted with a seemingly over-whelming situation: ruling the entire nation of Israel, God's chosen people. What does his approach say to us when we are confronted with overwhelming situations in our lives?
We will face such situations in our lives, and it is all right to be confronted with circumstances or decisions that seem overwhelming. What is important is that we acknowledge our limitations and seek the Lord and His guidance in the midst of them.

16. John 15:5 says, "I am the vine, you are the branches; he who abides in Me and I in him, he bears much fruit; for apart from Me you can do nothing." How do Solomon's actions indicate his understanding of this principle?
He knew that he would be unable to rule the people without the Lord's wisdom to guide him. Apart from God, he could do nothing. Solomon lived out this principle.

18. Why do you think God is pleased when we ask Him for wisdom?
In asking the Lord for wisdom, we are acknowledging our own lack of it. We also acknowledge our desire for God. God is pleased when we ask Him for those things that He wants for us as well.

20. How do you know when a person is wise?
Possible answers: When a person relies on the wisdom of the Lord and lives his or her life in line with God's Word, you know that he or she is wise. A wise person is able to give godly counsel to others. A wise person demonstrates understanding beyond what the "average" person would be able to discern, etc.

DAY 3

 **FOCUS**
Mankind seeks and puts forth great effort into obtaining the treasures of the earth without realizing the value of wisdom. Yet the Lord determined that wisdom, which is eternal, is of far greater value than temporal, earthly treasure. It is only through fearing the Lord that a person can begin to claim wisdom as his or her own possession.

APPLICATION
24. Man is willing to go where no one else has gone before and separate himself from other people in order to obtain the riches that the earth provides. What does this say about his motivation?
He is setting his desires on temporal things and values them to the extent that he is willing to separate himself from people, who are eternal. He gives his entire life to possessing the earth's treasures.

26. Although Job had been amply blessed with them, what value did he put on earthly treasures?
They had no value in comparison to godly wisdom and his relationship with God. The treasures of the world were not his priority.

27. The animals and birds live their lives in and around the earth, and yet they do not know the value of the earth's treasures. In what way are we like them?
We have such ready access to the Lord's wisdom and yet we do not know the value of it.

28. Wisdom cannot be found on the land or in the sea. Why is this true?
Wisdom cannot be found in worldliness or in the things of the world.

29. If a person who has sought riches discovers the value of the Lord's wisdom after death, what is the result?
Then it is too late. In death, all will realize what is truly valuable—God and His wisdom.

31. God set up the boundaries of the waters, put the world and the other planets in motion, and created air and rain and heat which sustain life. God holds everything in the universe together and all work in harmony. In light of this, how trustworthy is God's wisdom?

He has all knowledge and all power. His wisdom is vast, complete, and perfect. How could we not trust it?

33. If God's people put as much effort into obtaining wisdom as they do into obtaining the riches of the earth, what would be the result?
The result would be a godly nation whose collective heart was completely His. And because wisdom is eternal, its value far exceeds the brief existence of the earth and its treasures.

34. Fearing God means to revere Him, to hold Him in honor and esteem. Why do we only begin to gain wisdom when we fear Him?
When we revere Him, we do not put pride in ourselves, but instead acknowledge our own inadequacy and seek Him in humility. We cannot gain His wisdom any other way.

What is the result when people are wealthy but are not wise?
When this is the case, they do not use their wealth wisely. In many cases, they lose it even while on earth. They will certainly lose it in death.

DAY 4

 ## FOCUS
Wisdom is more valuable than any earthly treasure. God, in His infinite wisdom, created the heavens and earth. Therefore, we can trust His wisdom to guide us no matter how difficult the situation may seem. If we seek His wisdom, we can live our lives in the security of it.

 ## APPLICATION
38. When earthly matters and possessions dominate our list of the things we desire the most, how does it impact our desire for the things that are eternal?
When we make earthly treasures a priority, devoting our time and energy to obtaining them, our efforts in regard to eternal things are reduced or even eliminated all together. Earthly concerns serve as a diversion to the things that are truly important.

39. As we devote more time to pursuing the wisdom of the Lord, how do you think it will impact our view of worldly concerns?
We will begin to put them in the proper perspective. Wisdom will be far more valuable to us than precious jewels, new automobiles, a boyfriend or girlfriend, new sound systems, and designer clothing.

40. Many passages from the Bible describe the hand of God. In it are generosity (Psalm 145:16) security (John 10:29) and protection (Psalm 139:10) for example. Proverbs 3:16 says that in the hand of wisdom are long life, riches, and honor. Because God is the source of all of these things, what do we know about Him when it comes to wisdom?
In God's hand is wisdom. God is the source of it. Just as the hand is a part of the body, so wisdom is a divine attribute of the Lord. God is wisdom.

42. Why do you think we sometimes are overcome with feelings of uncertainty, defeat, and anxiety when we are about to start college, select a course of study, change schools, or start an after-school job?
We face these emotions when we are relying on our own wisdom to get us through difficult, challenging, and new situations. It is only when we are following the Lord's lead and allowing Him to take care of the details for us, relying on His wisdom and abilities instead of our own, that we are able to find security.

BRIDGES QUOTATION
Who is someone you are likely to seek out to listen to your concerns or to give you advice when you are agonizing over an important decision?
Possible answers: a close friend, a youth minister, a parent, your pastor, your team leader, a teacher, or a coach.

Although the Lord provides us with godly counsel in our relationships on earth, why should we seek His direction over the direction anyone else would instruct us to follow?
God sees the whole picture. If He is able to create the heavens and the earth out of nothing and bring life into existence, He is able to handle any dilemma or decision we might face. His wisdom is something we should seek because only His is perfect.

44. Verse 22 says that wisdom will be an adornment to your neck. How will others view your wisdom?
It will be attractive to them, just as a gold necklace around someone's neck is attractive.

What do verses 23-24 indicate will be the result if we choose not to seek the Lord's wisdom in our lives?
Our ways will be insecure, our feet will stumble, when we lie down we will face fears and we will not sleep in peace.

DAY 5

FOCUS

God is faithful to give us wisdom if we ask Him for it. True wisdom does not lie in reason or research, but in our relationship with God. If we want to be like Christ, we must know Him.

APPLICATION

MACLAREN QUOTATION

LIFE SITUATION

"What are you doing?" Jonathon asked his friend Grey as he peered over the book Grey was diligently reading.

"I'm looking for answers," Grey responded.

"Answers to what?"

Grey put his book down. "If you must know, I'm facing a tough decision and I want all of the facts before I make it."

"Okay, I give up. What's the big dilemma?" Jonathon questioned.

"I have to know whether I should study geology or speech therapy in college. I mean, it's just a few months away, and I can't just start without knowing my major! I'm interested in them both, you know, but I can't do them both. So I've been talking to my mom about it, and I asked Ms. Kincaid what she thinks."

"The counselor?" Jonathon asked.

"Yeah. And I'm trying to find out what kind of jobs I could get with either one. And I'm looking through college textbooks to see which one would be...well...more interesting. And I also talked to almost all of my teachers to see what they thought. And nearly everyone in my chemistry class thinks I would make a good speech therapist. But Mr. Escabar says he thinks science is my best area, but of course he would say that, considering he's a science teacher. And I've been looking at what colleges offer them, and..."

Grey is seeking a lot of advice. If he listens to everyone's well-intentioned suggestions, what will be the result?
The result will be confusion. More advice doesn't mean better advice.

If he wants to make the wisest decision, whose direction should he seek?

He should be seeking the Lord's wisdom, because He knows His plan for Grey's life and the path he needs to take to realize it (James 1:5).

46. When you are driving down the road, trying to find your way to a specific destination, you are looking for a sign—a street sign or road sign that will let you know you are headed in the right direction. When asking the Lord for direction, we are often seeking a sign. When we ask for wisdom instead of direction, however, what are we seeking?
When we ask for wisdom, we are seeking God.

What good does it do us to know which direction to take when we don't have the wisdom to know what to do once we get there?

Is the wisdom we seek limited to the immediate decision or situation?
Wisdom is not limited to one moment in time or one particular circumstance. Wisdom is ongoing.

48. What avenues might God choose to use in order to reveal His wisdom?
Godly counsel, circumstances, prayer, Scripture, etc.

50. True wisdom lies in knowing God. This underscores the inadequacy of earthly wisdom. In fact, how do the wise people of the earth, such as scientists and scholars, often view God?
They minimize Him or even deny Him. For example, evolutionists don't acknowledge God as the source of life. Many don't acknowledge His existence at all.

This year's emphasis in discipleship has been on becoming Christlike. In reality, the only way to become like Him is to know Him. It would be foolish to say that you wanted to be like someone that you knew absolutely nothing about. If you want to have integrity, should you read a book about it? If you want to be disciplined, should you take a course in self-discipline? If you want to love others, should you attend a seminar on the subject?
If you want to love God and others, want to walk in integrity, to have self-control, joy, and peace regardless of the circumstances, you must seek to know God.

WEEK 29
A MORE EXCELLENT WAY

DAY 1

FOCUS

Jesus demonstrated the greatest love in His life through selfless ministry to others and in His death through willingly laying down His life for sinners. While the world looks for love to be self-beneficial, God's love is unconditional, sacrificial, and pure.

APPLICATION

1. Indicate which of the following actions or attitudes would be characteristic of someone who loves you:
a. wants to spend time with you
b. is willing to sacrifice for you
c. wants the best for you even when it doesn't include him or her
d. treats you with respect
e. puts your feelings and needs above his or her own
f. rejoices in your successes
g. all of the above
Answer: g.

2. When a person says, "I love you," how can you know his or her words are a true reflection of how he or she really feels?
The best indication of whether or not the words "I love you" are sincere is whether or not the words are supported by actions that demonstrate them.

5. In our prayers, we often say the words, "I love you," to the Lord. How are our actions an affirmation of our words?

7. If Jesus had followed the traditional pattern of how young adults lived their lives, and still do, to what things would Jesus have devoted His energies?
He would have spent His time and energies building a home and making a good living. Instead, He had no home and didn't spend His time pursuing financial security. He devoted His entire life to holiness.

8. How was the reality of Jesus' death different from the two men who were crucified next to Him?
They were crucified because of what they did, because of the crimes they committed. Jesus was crucified for something He didn't do, but everyone else did. They didn't take His life from Him because He willingly gave it out of love for mankind.

9. In what ways is worldly love a selfish love?
Even when a person loves another, he or she makes requirements of the person. Does he or she meet my needs? Does he or she love me in return? Will he or she remain committed to me? And if these expectations are not met from someone the person claims to love, he or she is likely to look for love elsewhere.

LIFE SITUATION

Lulani hadn't seen her friend Teri in over a month. School was just getting ready to start back up and Lulani had recently returned from a vacation out West with her parents. She was a little bit anxious about her friend's emotional state. Just before Lulani left on her trip, Teri's boyfriend of six months, Kent, had broken up with her suddenly, for no reason. Teri was crushed. Lulani had been there for her friend when it happened. She had seen her tears and felt her heartache. Lulani was afraid now that school was starting back up, Teri would see her old boyfriend with his new girlfriend and it would stir up a lot of emotions. But Lulani would be there for her now, just like she was then.
"Who, Kent?" Lulani heard Teri respond to their friend Lucille as Lulani entered the cafeteria where they were sitting. "Yeah, I know he's dating Melia now. I think they've been together for nearly a month, as a matter of fact."
"So, like, you're OK with that?" asked Lucille.
"Yeah. I know it sounds strange. I mean, I loved him and all, and he said he loved me, but, you know, I really don't think much about him anymore. I mean, it was great while it lasted; isn't that what they say?"

"Teri! I'm so glad everything's okay!" Lulani told her friend as she gave her a hug.

"Yeah, it's kind of hard to believe I was that upset over the guy. I mean, it's cool with me if he's moved on, because so have I!" Teri and her friends laughed as she began telling them about the guy she met at the pool a few weeks ago...

During her relationship with Kent, what do you think led Teri to believe that she loved him?
More than likely, she based it on emotion—the elation of having a boyfriend and wanting to be with him most of the time.

When a person is in a long-term relationship, such as that of a husband and wife, and the emotion of love has changed from elation to comfortable steadiness, is it an indication that love is not as strong as it once was?
No. Not only is the love as strong as before, but then there exists the opportunity for love to deepen in its commitment and actions. It is an opportunity for love to experience new dimensions.

On what must the commitment of a long-term relationship be based?
It can't be based on the individuals, because they are sinners and will therefore fail each other. The commitment must be based on God's love for them and their love for Him.

10. The world says, "I love you if...." What does God's love say?
God's love says, "I love you eternally. No strings attached."

DAY 2

FOCUS
Paul characterizes love in 1 Corinthians 13. Even small deeds performed in love have great value, while great deeds done in the absence of love are worth nothing.

APPLICATION
13. What does it mean to "deliver your body to be burned"?
It means becoming a martyr: going to your death for the sake of Christ.

16. Which has greater value: making a glass of iced tea for your mother, motivated by love, or working in a soup kitchen for hours preparing food for hundreds of homeless people, but resenting every minute of it?
The small deed in love (making tea) has great value, and the large deed without love (feeding hundreds) has no value.

How do you know when your efforts are truly motivated by love? Is it when you give willingly and get nothing in return?
If we were to see Jesus, face to face, and He asked a task of us, small or great, our willingness and love toward performing that task would be great. When we see Christ's face in the person we are serving and put forth the same amount of energy as we would if we were serving Him, we know our efforts are truly motivated by love.

17. "I'm not going to give him gas money again. He never gives me money for gas when I drive."
"I really need to do something nice for her. She's always doing things for me."
"I'm not going to let him help me clean out the garage. I don't want to help him clean his out. It's ten times worse!"
What is wrong with these statements?
These people are not giving of themselves or serving out of love. Even when they are willing to do something for another person, it is done out of obligation.

What elements of love that Paul lists in this passage do you recognize from the following?
a. Judy made a near-perfect score on her ACT's, but didn't even mention it to her friend Shelly when Shelly told Judy about her own mediocre score.
(does not brag; is not arrogant)
b. Tameka walked away when the others in her group started telling "dirty" jokes.
(does not rejoice in unrighteousness)
c. Cathryn wanted to run for class president, but when she found out that her best friend Erika was running, she decided to try for a different office.
(does not seek its own)
d. Quint knew others talked about how insincere Conner really was, flattering others just so they would like him more, but Quint didn't view him as insincere. He thought he probably just liked to comment on people's strong points.
(believes all things; hopes all things)
e. Ronald knew that Enrique, a new Christian, had gone out drinking with his non-Christian friends again. This was the third time he had done it since he

had accepted Christ and vowed not to party anymore. Ronald decided to mention the incident to Enrique but to also encourage him in the areas in which he was showing growth and commitment and try to get him more involved in church-related activities. (patient; kind; is not provoked)

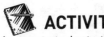

ACTIVITY

Instruct students to make up their own scenarios of interactions between people that reflect elements of love from this passage. They could also create scenarios in which peers are not demonstrating these elements. Time permitting, students could work as partners and role play their scenarios.

DAY 3

FOCUS

It is only possible to love the unlovely through abiding in Christ. Because all people are created in God's image, when we love others, we are loving Him. When we despise others, we are despising Him. We must see Christ in the faces of others and respond to them as we would respond to Him.

APPLICATION

DRUMMOND QUOTATION

You can't do it. You just can't love certain people. No matter how hard you try, there are people that just really rub you the wrong way. So what can you do? Should you work as hard as you can trying to love them? Should you convince yourself that you really do love them? Should you grit your teeth and be nice to them? If you try hard enough, do you think you eventually will love them?

There is no way we can possibly create within ourselves the capacity to love others. The only way this is possible is through devoting ourselves to Christ and falling in love with Him, so that His love for others becomes our love for them as well.

Genesis 1:27

God could have said that the evidence of our love for Him is in the way we treat animals or the respect we have for the environment. After all, He is the creator of all things. Why do you think, instead, He chose to emphasize our relationships with other people?

God confronts us with Himself in the faces of the people who were created in His own image.

26. Because all people are created in the image of God, we should see Him when we see them. Obviously, nonbelievers will be unable to do this. Yet how can we enable them to see Christ when they look at us?

They will see Him if we are like Him.

27. The word "hate" rolls off of our tongues with such ease, even when it is used to describe the way we feel about other people. When we choose to hate another person, with whom are we aligning ourselves?

We are aligning ourselves with Satan.

28. If you saw Christ in the face of your mother, how would that affect the way you talk to her?

You would talk to her with an attitude of respect and obedience.

If you saw Christ in the face of your enemy, how would that affect your relationship with him or her?

You would show unconditional love to him or her and would not hold a grudge.

If you saw Christ in the face of all of those people in the waiting room at the doctor's office who are causing you to have to wait longer, how would that affect your attitude toward them?

You would be happy to wait. You would be compassionate and concerned for their health and well-being instead of focusing solely on your own concerns.

31. What will you do the next time you...

...have to taxi your sister all over town?

...have to stand in line at the cafeteria for 15 minutes because the cashier is new at the job?

...run in to the guy who is spreading false rumors about you all over school?

...make a B on a term paper you really deserved an A on because you aren't one of your "teacher's pets"?

The next time, try seeing Christ in the face of the person who has inconvenienced you, taken advantage of you, or been unfair to you.

DAY 4

FOCUS

Just as God's love for us was confirmed when He gave His Son to die for us, so our love is confirmed when we lay down our lives for others through selfless action.

 **APPLICATION**

33. What emotions well up within us when we entertain hatred in our hearts for another person?
Possible answers: bitterness, anger, hostility, frustration, or vengeance.

Are these emotions and thoughts promoting to life or to death?
Death. Those who harbor hatred and all of the emotions that go with it quench the Spirit within them.

38. How can you back up the words "I love you" with action in your relationships with...
...your parents?
Possible answers: helping out around the house willingly, respecting authority, and not making demands for material things.
...your grandparents?
Possible answers: spending time with them, listening to them talk about "the good old days", helping them with upkeep on their house or lawn.
...your best friend?
Possible answers: helping him with a class assignment, treating her to a movie, or listening to him.
...your boyfriend/girlfriend?
Possible answers: putting his or her needs before your own, treating him or her with respect, or not tempting him or her to compromise moral standards.

41. What about the person who already has every possible material need met? Shouldn't that person be laying down his or her life in the form of helping you out every now and then?
Emotional needs and spiritual needs must be met as well. It is when a person doesn't seem to have any needs that we must look deeper into the emotional and spiritual aspects of his or her life.

43. "I want to do more for others, but I'm so busy." How many times have we said the same thing? Taking into consideration the classwork, part-time jobs, extracurricular activities, and church activities, how can anyone blame us for not being more willing to love others through our actions? We would like to, we just don't have the time right now. Is it good enough just to want to help others, even if the actual deeds will have to wait until summer vacation?
The problem is that we use our lack of time as an excuse to pack our schedules with everything that relates to, concerns, and benefits us. Sometimes it just comes down to giving something up so that we can serve someone else.

DAY 5

 FOCUS

People obey the law because they will be punished if they don't. Love sets us free from the law and even exceeds it because it desires only the best for others. When confronted with those who do not love us back, we begin to experience the same thing Christ experiences in loving people.

APPLICATION

45. The law doesn't motivate us to exceed its requirements. In fact, what does the law actually motivate us to do?
It encourages us to find loopholes so we will have to pay as little as possible.

How is this like our commitment to love when it comes to others?
We are likely to love others as much as is required of us and no more. We give only when it doesn't require sacrifice. We love if it is reciprocated. We love if the other person is worthy of it.

When we love, we don't "do good" to others because we fear punishment if we don't. We don't think in terms of the benefits or consequences. Yet what could be the penalty we might pay when we love others?

The penalty could be not getting love back in return. This was the penalty Christ paid for His love.

49. What other godly attributes are a result of love?
All are a result of love: compassion, mercy, forgiveness, and gentleness.

LEWIS QUOTATION
Those people who choose to sin and reject our love actually fulfill a significant purpose in our lives. Jesus was confronted with those who chose sin, taking from Him and others and giving nothing in return. What can we understand about Christ that we would not know if we never met such people?
When we continue to love such people, we are sharing in the fellowship of Christ's sufferings (Phil. 3:10) and we are learning what He experiences in loving those who reject and even deny Him. If we were not confronted with such people in our own lives, we would never be able to understand the selfless, unconditional nature of His love.

WEEK 30
A CALL TO OBEDIENCE

DAY 1

 ### FOCUS

Obedience to the Lord means keeping His commandments. Our love for God is revealed by our obedience to Him, and it is this obedience that is required if we are to truly have an intimate relationship with Him.

 ### APPLICATION

2. What is the difference between obeying someone because you love him or her and obeying because you are afraid of being punished if you don't? Isn't the end result the same: obedience?

The motive to our obedience reveals a great deal about the condition of our heart, and the Lord knows our heart. Obedience because we are afraid of punishment is improperly motivated obedience, and when it is the reason for our obedience to God, it reveals an inaccurate concept of His divine nature. When you obey a person because you are afraid of the consequences if you don't obey, once that threat is removed, the result will be disobedience.

4. Knowing God's laws must precede obeying them. What do you think is the result when someone not only knows God's laws, but knows God as well?

The result is a person who loves God and obeys Him because of it. That is the significance of our obedience. Our love for God is revealed by whether or not we obey Him.

8. When others know we claim to love God, know we attend church regularly, and know we listen to Christian music, but they also know that our lives are not any different in terms of obedience to God's commands than those of nonbelievers, what conclusions will they draw about Christians?

They probably know that our claims are superficial. They probably know we don't truly love Him at all.

DAY 2

 ### FOCUS

We know Jesus lives in our hearts if we keep His commandments. An obedient lifestyle is the evidence of eternal life because actions reveal what is on the heart. We must obey in humility, and our obedience must be based on our love for God. Head knowledge in the absence of heart knowledge is worthless.

APPLICATION

11. Many people come to God on their terms and not on His. They will attend church, if it fits into their schedules. They will read the Bible, if they have a few extra minutes. They will pray in times of need. But they will also party with their friends, hate their enemies, and lie to their parents if the need arises. What is true of the person who comes to God only on his or her own terms?

He or she hasn't come to God at all. We come to Him on His terms, not ours. That is why not everyone who says to Him "Lord, Lord," will enter the kingdom of heaven (Matthew 7:21). A person might think he or she is a Christian (and many do) but the truth is in the action.

12. Although we may tend to rank the specific sins listed in Galatians 5:19-21, what is true about them?

They are all sin, and they are all equally detestable in the sight of God. We tend to generalize obedience in terms of the big things. But every act or word or thought is one of either obedience or disobedience, based on our choices.

All Christians sin. But when does sin begin to reveal the absence of Christ in the life of a person who claims to be a Christian?

When a person rejects God's laws in favor of sin, enjoys sinning, and has little or no remorse afterward, Christ is not in him or her. (1 John 2:4)

Titus 1:16
What is true of the good deeds performed by those who profess to be Christians but blatantly rebel against God's commands?
They are worthless.

17. How is the relationship between obedience and holiness like the relationship between flour and bread?
Just as you cannot make bread without flour, so you cannot be holy without being obedient.

19. What is true of obedience that is based on...
...the desire for the favorable recognition of others?
...the desire to avoid punishment?
...the desire to feel spiritually "superior" to others?
None is obedience that is pleasing to God. Obedience based on our humble desire to live up to what He has given us by grace and that is motivated by our love for Him is the obedience that honors God, and that God honors. (1 Peter 5:6)

21. How do we make the transition from intellectual knowledge to spiritual application? If we work hard enough and try our best, can we do it?
The only way to take on the qualities of Christ and make them a reality in our own lives is to get close to the source of them. We need to spend time with God in order to become like Him.

22. James gives us an accurate picture of the level of usefulness of intellectual knowledge. He tells us that hearers who are not doers delude themselves (James 1:22), and that even the demons believe. In fact, they have as much knowledge as we do (James 2:19). So when we live by intellectual knowledge alone, instead of walking in integrity, love, gentleness, etc., what are examples of attributes in which we are walking?
Possible answers: hypocrisy, laziness, self centeredness, pride, or foolishness.

DAY 3

 ## FOCUS
Good deeds that do not originate in the will of God, in the midst of obedience, are rejected by Him. Obedience is the proof that a person has trusted Christ because it can only be accomplished when the heart is right and, because of the sin nature, when it is empowered by the Holy Spirit. Delayed obedience is disobedience.

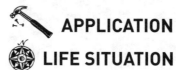 ## APPLICATION
LIFE SITUATION
Seong is just a kid, really. And just like any other kid, occasionally he rebels. So what if he cheats on his tests every now and then and spends a lot of his weekends partying with the rowdy crowd? He's not an adult, after all. He's just having fun. Everyone expects teenagers to rebel now and then. It's nobody's fault. They just have to sow their wild oats. They'll get over it. Seong will get over it. He'll have some fun now, and later, when he's grown up, he'll straighten up. He'll obey God then. He'll be more mature then, ready to settle down. After high school, or maybe college, he'll follow God. After all, right now he's just a kid.

What do you think is Seong's level of commitment to God?
He is not committed to following God. He is committed to pursuing sin.

What do you think will happen to Seong's commitment once he is out of high school?
There will always be another reason for Seong to delay being obedient to God. It might not be in the form of blatant sin, but it could be a matter of not really seeking or even including God in his life. Seong doesn't need to grow up. What he needs is a change of heart.

OGILVIE QUOTATION
If we want the Lord to show us His will for our life, His purpose for our future, what should we be doing in terms of our relationship with Him today?
We should be obeying His commands. If we want Him to reveal His will for our future to us, we need to be trustworthy with what He has already revealed to us in terms of His will for our lives (that we obey Him).

DAY 4

 ## FOCUS
Nadab and Abihu, the sons of Aaron, were consumed with fire from the Lord when they offered Him an unauthorized sacrifice. We must come to God on His terms and not on our own. Before their sin, Nadab and Abihu, even in their youth, were set apart as priests. God has created great potential for the years of youth, so we must strive to obey Him regardless of our age.

APPLICATION

35. How did Aaron, the father of Nadab and Abihu, demonstrate his own obedience in this situation?
When the Lord caused Nadab and Abihu to be consumed by fire because of their disobedience, Aaron did not question the Lord or become angry, nor did he rebel or even grieve. He remained silent.

36. How has God called His people to a higher standard of obedience?
If we are His children, we must treat Him with honor and reverence. It is expected that an unbeliever will live a life of sin, but those who come near to Him must treat Him as holy.

39. What are examples of people in the Bible who accomplished great things even when they were young because they were living in the will of the Lord?
David was only a youth when he became a national hero by killing the Philistine giant, Goliath. Timothy was very young when he became one of Paul's greatest comrades in spreading the gospel. Mary was barely a teenager when she gave birth to Jesus.

Young people often obtain positions of leadership in the church, such as leading Bible studies. Many people hear the call to vocational ministry during adolescence. Age is not an issue when it comes to obedience, nor is reaching a certain age a prerequisite to serving Him, seeking Him, and knowing Him. What is the only requirement to being used of God?
We must be willing to obey Him and yield to His will. God can use anyone who is willing to accomplish His purpose.

DAY 5

 FOCUS
God gives us the desire to obey Him. The only way to bring the will of our sin nature under control is by abiding in Christ. If we seek Him, He will give us victory over our sin nature.

 APPLICATION
42. How has the presence of your team leader affected your obedience to God in working out your salvation?
He or she is a source of accountability. Your team leader is someone who asks you about your

Scripture memory and studies, your attitudes toward your friends, teachers, and classes; your relationship with your parents, etc. When you see your team leader, it makes you think about God, His requirements, and your relationship with Him.

43. Team leaders and other adult discipleship leaders will not always be there to offer you support and accountability when it comes to your relationship with God. Regardless of the number of people that surround you, what is really true about your relationship with Him?
It is really just you and God and no one else. He is the One to whom you are accountable. You cannot depend on your team leader or any other person to be the channel between you and God.

It is God who gives us the desire...
How do we bring our will into control? We want to pray that God will overcome our will and make us obey Him, but He doesn't work that way. The Lord tells us what to do before He will rain His righteousness on us. Hosea 10:12 says, "Sow with a view to righteousness, reap in accordance with kindness; Break up your fallow ground, for it is time to seek the Lord until He comes to rain righteousness on you." Where do you start if you lack the desire to obey Him?
You must start by meeting with Him. If you stay away from God, your will will be overcome by the sin nature. Breaking up our fallow ground means not playing the game of Christianity: church on Sunday and sin every other day. It means seeking God, learning from Him, learning of Him, daily. In knowing God, we cannot help but love Him. It is then that obedience to Him becomes the desire of our hearts.

"It is written in the prophets, 'And they shall all be taught of God.' Everyone who has heard and learned from the Father comes to Me." John 6:45

Plug-in and Transform Students... with These User friendly Products!

Add a strong foundation to your True Love Waits efforts by seizing these exciting and relevant in-depth student resources.

True Love Waits Takes a Look at Courting, Dating, and Hanging Out
by David Payne
This new and very cool resource transforms students' views of courtship, dating, and hanging out. The approach is fun, honest, and spiritually provocative. No youth group should miss the biblically correct activities packed into this study. 5 sessions. Easy plan. Just add students. Each book includes an exclusive study for male and female participants.
ISBN 0-6330-0463-4, $4.95

Sexual Resolutions
by Paul Kelly
A core belief in True Love Waits is a desire to see girls and guys treat each other with respect and dignity. This resource is a great place to start. Words like respect, honesty, purity, and Christ-like living are the backbone of this easy-to-use study.
ISBN 0-6330-0289-5, $2.95

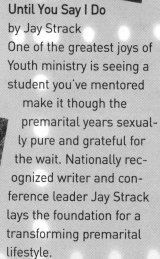

Until You Say I Do
by Jay Strack
One of the greatest joys of Youth ministry is seeing a student you've mentored make it though the premarital years sexually pure and grateful for the wait. Nationally recognized writer and conference leader Jay Strack lays the foundation for a transforming premarital lifestyle.
The words and activities of this resource are a great way to take youth into a new understanding of marriage preparation.
ISBN 0-7673-3181-8, $3.95

The Relationship Revolution
by Rodney Gage
Are you ready to start a revolution? Through learning how to best understand and help their friends, many teens will see emotional needs that are unmet in their own lives and develop ways to help themselves as well.
ISBN 0-7673-9868-8, $9.95

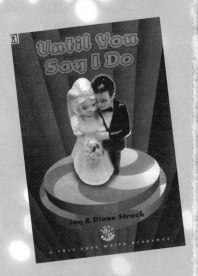

To order these resources: **WRITE** LifeWay Church Resources Customer Service, 127 Ninth Avenue, North, Nashville, TN 37234-0113; **FAX** order to (615) 251-5933; **PHONE** 1-800-458-2772; **EMAIL** to CustomerService@lifeway.com; **ONLINE** at www.lifeway.com; or visit the LifeWay Christian Store serving you.

LifeWay®
Church Resources